D0046421

COMEBACK
AMERICA

COMEBACK
AMERICA

Turning the Country Around
and Restoring Fiscal Responsibility

DAVID M. WALKER

RANDOM HOUSE 🏠 NEW YORK

Copyright © 2009 by Peter G. Peterson Foundation

All rights reserved.

Published in the United States by Random House,
an imprint of The Random House Publishing Group,
a division of Random House, Inc., New York.

RANDOM HOUSE and colophon are registered
trademarks of Random House, Inc.

Library of Congress Cataloging-in-Publication Data

Walker, David M. (David Michael).
Comeback America : turning the country around and restoring fiscal
responsibility / David M. Walker.
p. cm.
ISBN 978-1-4000-6860-9
eBook ISBN 978-1-58836-976-5
1. Fiscal policy—United States.   2. Financial crises—United
States—History—21st century.   3. United States—Economic
conditions—2009–   4. Global Financial Crisis, 2008–2009.
I. Title.
HJ275.W235   2009
330.973—dc22   2009037968

Printed in the United States of America
on acid-free paper

www.atrandom.com

2 4 6 8 9 7 5 3 1

First Edition

Book design by Liz Cosgrove

For my family,
the Peter G. Peterson Foundation,
and my fellow citizens

Contents

Prologue

America is a great country—the greatest, as far as Americans are concerned. But its future is threatened, and we same Americans are the threat. I am talking about our nation's deteriorating financial condition, perpetrated by all of us, and especially by the government that represents us. It is easy to ignore this national decline. Even in these hard times, we see relative prosperity and unparalleled power all around us. But the danger is there even if we fail to acknowledge it. The American way of life will go downhill, steadily and inexorably, unless we do something about our growing fiscal imbalance—and do it soon.

I think you already realize that we are in a lot of trouble. After all, you have just picked up a book on the fiscal crisis by a certified public accountant and the government's former top auditor. If you find yourself concerned about how our nation is spending money it doesn't have, and spending it unwisely, then you have the right instinct. You should be worried. And this book might make you even more worried. But it will also show you a way out of the huge hole our elected officials have dug us into.

We have run deficits over the course of our history for a variety of reasons, from paying for wars, to fighting the Great Depression, to stimulating the economy in times of recession. But in the past thirty years, America and many Americans have become addicted to debt and to conspicuous consumption. As the baby-boom generation gets older and the growth of our workforce slows, we will pay more for Social Security, Medicare, and other programs that already dominate our budget. And we will find it harder and harder to pay for this spending. It's like having a credit card. At first, you pay off most or all of the balance. But as you continue to spend, the balance grows, and so does the interest on that balance. Before long you're struggling just to pay the interest, and you have less money available for everything else. As we've seen all too often over the past few years, this pattern leads to bankruptcy.

We live in a great and resilient nation. For all of our problems, the United States remains a global superpower and a beacon of liberty for people around the world. We have much to be proud of and thankful for. But I am here to tell you that if we don't find a way to get spending under control, we will put our nation's economy and international standing at risk and bequeath to our children a world of severely diminished opportunities. But I'm also here to tell you that it's not too late, and that's what inspired me to write this book. I didn't call it "Comeback America" for nothing. We can make tough choices to restore fiscal sanity and stage a comeback from the recent financial crisis that has knocked us down. More important, we can come back to our basic principles and values, including thrift, personal responsibility, saving, and our stewardship obligation to shape a future for the next generation that is better than our past.

It will take a lot of hard work. In the pages that follow, I will tell you how we can take that spending machine off autopilot and redirect it to provide the services our nation needs at a price we can afford. That is going to involve dramatically rethinking our social programs, reforming our tax system and other spending programs, changing the way our government operates, and reforming our political system. And all this will happen only if "We the People" use the power of our democracy to force change from our elected officials.

Who am I to be sounding off? I spent fifteen years in Washington, working during four presidential administrations (Reagan, Bush 41, Clinton, and Bush 43). All my jobs involved working with top elected and appointed officials while also collaborating with a range of highly educated and dedicated civil servants—and all of them gave me a scary education in how our political system has failed to guard our nation's financial health.

I watched the Reagan revolution from my position as assistant secretary of labor for pension and welfare benefits. President Reagan cut taxes and increased defense spending simultaneously, which added billions to the government's budget deficit. Of course, there's an argument to be made that Reagan's defense buildup gave the Soviet Union a decisive push into oblivion, winning the Cold War without firing a shot. That in turn allowed us to cut defense spending (measured as a percentage of the national economy) and to enjoy a peace dividend of growth and creativity throughout our economy.

When we came down from that high induced by peace and lower taxes, however, we saw that the economic growth Reagan stimulated did not make up for the tax revenue we lost. As a consequence, our deficits were growing out of control.

I served under Reagan's successor, Bush 41, as one of two public trustees for the Social Security and Medicare systems. That job gave me a lot of insight into our money-draining social programs, which I'll share with you later. It also gave me a lifelong respect for our first President Bush, who had the courage to break a campaign promise—"Read my lips: No new taxes"—when he saw our deficits rising to the danger level. That decision probably cost him reelection, but it was the right decision for America. He also imposed tough budget controls to constrain spending and the expansion of government.

Let me also tip my hat to Ross Perot, the Texas businessman

who ran for president in 1992 and 1996. Perot was the only national candidate in my memory who faced the American people
with charts and graphs to pound home the point that the politicians in Washington were driving America into bankruptcy with
their loose-spending ways. He made fighting the deficit sexy, at
least for a while. He also showed that you don't have to win to
make a big difference.

Perot made it extremely hard for the man who defeated him,
Bill Clinton, to be anything less than fiscally responsible. I give
President Clinton and his Treasury secretary, Bob Rubin, a lot of
credit. They pushed through continuation of the statutory budget
controls first put in place by Bush 41. "Statutory" means that *by
law* Congress could not create new spending programs, among
other things, without ensuring that they were adequately funded.
Clinton set a good example for fiscal responsibility during his administration. He did not cut taxes, even though he had promised
to do so for the middle class. He did not expand entitlement programs or move to increase social spending; in fact, he saved money
through his welfare reforms.

Clinton also was very lucky. He was blessed with a strong economy powered by the high-tech boom. His tax and spending discipline, combined with high growth, boosted federal revenues to
their highest level (as a percentage of the economy) in history. In
2000, as he prepared to turn over the White House to Bush 43, the
U.S. government reported its first true budget surplus in more than
thirty years.

My higher education in these issues began in 1998, when Clinton nominated me to serve a fifteen-year term as the seventh comptroller general of the United States and CEO of what was then
called the General Accounting Office. That agency was responsible
for auditing the federal government's consolidated financial statements and for making sure Washington was accountable to the
people who pay the bills. (Six years into my term, we pushed

through an act of Congress, signed by President Bush, that, among other things, changed the agency's name to the Government Accountability Office, or GAO.)

I applied for the job because I wanted to maximize my ability to make a difference for my fellow citizens (certainly not to maximize my net worth, since it required me to take a pay cut of more than 80 percent). I couldn't have asked for a better time than the late 1990s to take this watchdog role. But the flush times, of course, didn't last. After all the work it took to bring the deficit to zero, Washington seemed directionless. What do you do with a budget surplus? The answer is that you use it to build a new culture of fiscal responsibility. Once a balanced budget becomes the norm, you can begin to come to grips with the out-of-control social spending that leads to rising deficits and increasing debt levels.

But that's not how the new crowd in Washington looked at it. In 2001, Bush 43 came to town and joined the Republican Congress in proposing major tax cuts. The surplus was "the people's money," they reasoned, and should be returned to the people.

That kind of talk immediately made me somewhat nervous. In February 2001, less than a month after Bush took the oath of office, I went up to Capitol Hill and tried to instill a little fear, or at least some responsibility, into the Senate Budget Committee. I reminded the senators that it wasn't as simple as just giving the people back money in the form of tax cuts or adding new social programs. They had to consider future demands. The 77 million baby boomers born after World War II—one-fourth of the U.S. population—would start becoming eligible for Social Security in 2008 and for Medicare a few years after that. These programs were nowhere near well enough funded to handle the coming surge of spending, and we had to recognize that.

We shouldn't drop our guard, I warned the senators. Future budget surpluses were projected, but they may or may not actually materialize. Without continued financial discipline and without serious reforms in our social programs, I told them, demographics and escalating health care costs would overwhelm the surplus and drive us back into escalating deficits and debt. Our budget policy should cover all contingencies, I suggested. If the federal bottom line exceeded an established range, we could give taxpayers a dividend. If it fell short of our needs, we could impose a surcharge.

The committee's chairman, Pete Domenici (R) of New Mexico, had chided me for harping on the need for fiscal prudence when the senators were more concerned about how to spend the surplus. Several years later, he publicly conceded that he was wrong and encouraged me to harp away.

The Clinton surplus melted away even faster than I could have imagined. President Bush pushed through a tax cut in 2001—and the next year, and the year after that. The tax cuts came even as we mobilized for military campaigns in Afghanistan and Iraq and a global war against terror after 9/11. And they came despite Bush's decision to also push through a costly new Medicare drug benefit in 2003. As a result of these actions and other factors, the budget surplus that had been charted to last at least a decade disappeared almost overnight. We went from a $236 billion surplus in fiscal year 2000 to a deficit that was approaching $400 billion in fiscal 2003. The surplus was gone, and so was my patience.

When Bush 43 came to office, in 2001, he probably thought that I would be friendly to his administration, given my past appointments by his father and President Reagan. But as a nonpartisan professional, I thought the one-party government of the Bush-Cheney administration made both the GAO's role and my role as comptroller general even more important. If we didn't provide an objective view, then who in government would?

As the Bush administration geared up for the war against terror after 9/11, the GAO and I fought to keep its policies transparent. We even sued Vice President Cheney for the records associated with the National Energy Policy Development Group, which he headed, in part to try to keep the administration from creating secret White House task forces.

I wasn't happy with having to file suit, but our efforts to reach a reasonable resolution were rejected—ultimately, by Cheney himself in a phone conversation with me. So we exercised our legal rights. A Bush 43–appointed federal district court judge ruled against us on procedural grounds, but our unprecedented action and the ensuing publicity did result in greater transparency. The Bush administration never again denied us access to records during my tenure.

From the start, the Bush administration was challenging an even more fundamental principle, in my view—the government's duty to be a fiscally responsible steward of the American people's wealth and well-being. I can still recall sitting in the office of a senior congressional leader in the autumn of 2003 silently seething as he made clear that even after Bush's serial tax cuts and spending increases, Congress was going to pass the hugely expensive new prescription drug benefit for Medicare that Bush had championed. That's when something snapped in me. I would not, I promised myself, behave like a typical comptroller general.

Comptrollers general usually work in relative obscurity overseeing the churning-out of GAO reports for Congress. Our job is to produce the reports and recommendations; it's up to elected and appointed officials to act on them. But in late 2003, I decided to forget the securities of bureaucratic custom. I would keep on testifying in congressional hearing rooms and presiding over GAO reports—but I would also start going public about the massive rip-off these politicians were about to perpetrate mainly to make themselves look good as the 2004 elections approached. Here we go again, I thought, cutting taxes, increasing spending, and fobbing off the bill on our children and grandchildren.

Not only was the country going to war without declaring it, and without getting the consent of Americans to help pay for it, but Washington was poised to add on a huge new health care spending program while hiding behind the fantasy that it would somehow pay for itself. I had bought into the GAO's core values of accountability, integrity, and reliability, and I decided to use my office as a bully pulpit to call attention to the growing problem. I scheduled a speech at the National Press Club in September 2003 that would be covered by C-SPAN and National Public Radio— not the biggest of audiences, but highly influential. It was called "Truth and Transparency," and it can be found on the GAO's website at www.gao.gov.

The trick was to turn up my rhetoric without going so far that I sounded crazy. The growing deficit numbers alone made my case. I told the reporters and the wider audience assembled that day that in less than ten years we would be hit by a huge demographic tidal wave, one unprecedented in our nation's history, and one that could swamp our ship of state. "Many believe that we will ulti- mately act to address this imbalance, but when will we start?" I said. "Other nations have already started to address their long- range imbalances. When will we?" I managed, just barely, to re- frain from beating on the lectern.

Was anybody out there listening? Thankfully, yes. I got enough calls and emails from people—including many in high places—to suggest that Americans were looking for leadership on our finan- cial predicament, and that they weren't getting it from politicians. At the GAO we continued to sound the klaxons in strongly worded reports. In December 2004 I held a comptroller general's forum at the agency on our long-term fiscal challenge. I reached out beyond the usual deficit hawks and attracted a broad, nonpar- tisan coalition. Government officials; business, labor, and non- profit leaders; public opinion researchers; think-tank scholars; and journalists joined us at the fiscal future forum. Former commerce secretary Peter G. Peterson, chairman of the Blackstone Group, a multibillion-dollar private equity firm, attended. So did former

Federal Reserve chairman Paul Volcker; Bob Bixby, executive director of the Concord Coalition, a grassroots organization that advocates fiscal responsibility; and high-level representatives from various important organizations, including AARP.

The group agreed that our nation's finances were worse than advertised and that tough choices were needed. A number of us saw ourselves as the center of a nationwide movement that could shake our political leaders back to their senses. We decided to spread the word like country preachers, traveling to the far corners of our nation on a campaign we called the Fiscal Wake-Up Tour, which kicked off in the autumn of 2005.

The tour was supported by the Concord Coalition, the Brookings Institution and the Heritage Foundation—the leading liberal and conservative think tanks, respectively—and the GAO. We ventured out to spread the word about our coming fiscal meltdown in any available forum. I attended every meeting and Bob Bixby attended the vast majority, while scholars from Brookings (Belle Sawhill, Alice Rivlin, Paul Cullinan, Diane Rogers, and Doug Elmendorf), Heritage (Stuart Butler, Alison Fraser, and Brian Riedl), and other organizations (Maya MacGuineas, Joe Minarik, Will Marshall, and Andrew Biggs) joined us at various stops. I was the dark-suited preacher in rimless glasses, spouting facts, fire, and brimstone. Bob was more disheveled and used a more informal and humorous style to convey the folly of Washington's ways. We were very different, but made a good team.

I was the fast-paced and superorganized one, burning out a BlackBerry after a few months and earning the nickname First-Flight Dave. (If you want to be sure of taking off, always schedule yourself on the first flight of the day, even if it's before dawn on a frozen New Hampshire morning—especially then.) Bob was more unstructured and easygoing, though not about everything. Just ask the Concord staffers who had to scrounge around small-town America looking for Tab, the soft drink popular in the 1970s that he couldn't live without. He also smoked small cigars; try finding a hotel these days that allows those.

Our inaugural appearance was at the University of Richmond, in Virginia. Business and community leaders came to breakfast to hear us tell them that the nation's financial condition was worse than anyone let on and that they had to help us do something about it. Selling financial responsibility to a generation addicted to credit cards and conspicuous consumption is not the easiest job in the world, but we could tell by their reaction that our audience got it. One man stood up and asked us, "Who put us in this condition?" I wished I could have pointed to just one person or political party, but that wouldn't have been fair or accurate.

About twenty-five people attended that first business and community leaders' meeting. At our next meeting at the university, forty to fifty people showed up in a hall that could have held two hundred. We had hoped to attract young people to our cause, but we learned, brilliantly, that you can't schedule your meeting on the far side of campus during morning class hours and expect students to attend.

We got our act together pretty quickly. We started piggybacking our presentations on meetings of clubs such as the Kiwanis and Rotary that already attracted big crowds. Our target audiences were receptive. Business leaders knew finance and understood the numbers. The media began showing up, especially after the economy started going south. And we kept our focus on universities, believing that young people needed to know what their elders were up to. It didn't take them long to realize, once they got the facts, that they were being "screwed," as they typically put it.

After Richmond, we visited the Humphrey Institute of Public Affairs at the University of Minnesota, where we attracted more than a hundred to a town hall session and met with a number of student leaders. We really started to hit our stride at our stop in Kansas City, where six hundred people showed up for the public meeting. We also landed a sit-down with the editorial board of *The Kansas City Star,* which cosponsored our visit.

After we got our act down, Bob and I would swoop into a town with our other panelists like a fiscal SWAT team. I would fly in on the day of our presentation, hopefully booking "government first-class"—an aisle seat in the more spacious exit row of the economy section—and be gone either late that night or on the first flight the next morning. We would do our tag-team act for local audiences. We even started attracting the interest of celebrities, including Warren Beatty, Morgan Fairchild, and Tom Hanks. We would think up sound bites for the media—which became sharper as the economy sank and the deficit soared. "America now owes more than Americans are worth" was a good one. My call to "fight for America's future" had a nice patriotic ring to it as well, and I meant it.

Our movement was catching on. But timing is everything. It turned out that our nation was heading into the most destructive financial crisis in decades. From our perspective, the recession of 2008 was a double-edged sword. Yes, it gave us bigger audiences, people who wanted to hear about how the crisis would affect them. But their fears made them more focused on surviving today rather than on planning for tomorrow. I found myself devoting 90 percent of my time to contemporary issues, but I insisted on reserving at least 10 percent to focus on the future. I would tell audiences that the conditions that caused the subprime crisis also existed in the federal government's finances, and conclude by saying, "The only differences are the scale, and no one will bail out America!"

Our Fiscal Wake-Up Tour did not target the party in power, but always that eight-hundred-pound gorilla sitting just offstage: the growing gap between the cost of government and the promises that it made on one hand, and the money that was available to pay for those expenses on the other. I viewed it as my job to get those in charge to recognize their profligate ways, and I became more and more insistent as federal deficits, debt levels, foreign dependency, and the unfunded promises for Social Security and Medicare grew under the Bush 43 administration.

There was a personal side to my campaign that I did not often share with my audiences. My family, the Walkers, came to America in the 1680s. Some of my direct ancestors fought and died in the American Revolution, and I am now an officer in the Sons of the American Revolution. Every American shares ownership in our country, but for me, this connection is a very old, rich family affair, enhanced by my own service in government. When I fight for America's future, I'm thinking not only of myself and my wife, Mary, but of our children, Carol and Andy, and our three grandchildren, Christi, Grace, and Danny.

I believe that my frequent congressional testimonies and speeches and our adventures on the Fiscal Wake-Up Tour helped the cause. Between September 2005 and the election of 2008, our traveling road show visited more than forty cities. I visited many more in my capacity as comptroller general and in my next job, CEO of the Peter G. Peterson Foundation. In four years, I traveled to forty-five states, with one more scheduled by the end of 2009. I plan to speak in the remaining four states in 2010. My latest speech before turning this book in for publication was at Boise State University, where over 1,200 people attended and the NBC local affiliate taped the event for later broadcast. My message was always the same—promoting fiscal responsibility and the need to confront the tough choices ahead.

My official position in Washington gave me an opportunity to speak out and be heard. My problem was that it didn't give me the power to propose specific policy reforms, to write books, to appear in the media as much as I felt was necessary, or to lead an aggressive grassroots campaign designed to hold elected officials accountable for what they did, or what they failed to do.

Fortunately, I had met Pete Peterson prior to the start of the Fiscal Wake-Up Tour. After years of championing fiscal responsibility, Pete pledged to start his own foundation after Blackstone went public. He decided to dedicate his time, talent, and treasure to help save America's future. The foundation's sole purpose would be to spotlight America's growing economic challenges and take steps designed to accelerate action on them. In March 2008, I left the GAO to head the Peterson Foundation, in large part in order to be able to partner with Pete.

Since joining Pete's foundation, I've been making my speeches, appearing on TV, writing op-ed articles, showing the foundation's movie (titled *I.O.U.S.A.*), building a new organization, and now writing this book. Let me add here that this book is based primarily on my experience as comptroller general. The views I express in these pages represent my personal observations and analysis, and not necessarily the views of the Peter G. Peterson Foundation. All my speaking fees go to the foundation, as will the royalties from this book.

I hope this book will achieve three goals. The first is to explain our fiscal predicament in a way that allows everyone, regardless of how comfortable they are with math or finance, to understand it. Second, I want to draw a road map out of this mess. And third, I want to offer readers the tools with which to evaluate programs going forward. When the president or members of Congress propose programs that are supposedly "fair" and "pay for themselves," the Americans who read this book will be able to ask the right skeptical and probing questions.

It is our duty to keep close watch on our government. We are shareholders in the American republic and we must be stewards of the future. We must hold the board (the Congress) and the management (the administration) accountable for their actions and for their failures to act. After all, each American generation has an obligation to leave the country better off and better positioned for those who come after us. From generation to generation, we must shore up our financial security, which is essential to the strength of our nation. That's a vital responsibility, in my view, that we have largely forgotten. It's time to bring it back.

As we come out of the current recession, we will be tempted to resume life as it was at the beginning of 2007. To do so would be a big mistake. Instead, we should start to ask ourselves important questions about our future. When we pass on, what will we leave for our kids and grandkids? What would you want to give them, a bequest or a burden? Would you really want to give them a credit card with a huge balance that you and the federal government accumulated and they have to pay off?

I know you will agree that we need to find another way. The ideas I'll give you in this book are illustrations. You will have your own ideas, and we should consider lots of options together. Help me get this nation's priorities straight so that we can bequeath a thriving nation to our descendants, as our parents did to us. I'm the accountant, but all of us can add and subtract. Now can we teach Washington how to do that?

COMEBACK
AMERICA

One

FISCAL CRISIS 101

When you give a speech, you're usually trying to deliver a few applause lines and maybe a laugh or two. But when I went out on the road to talk about America's financial crisis, I counted my talk successful if it induced something else: shocked silence.

It wasn't that hard to pull off. All I had to do was deliver a few jarring facts. "Our country is in a $56 trillion financial hole as of September 30, 2008," I would tell my audiences. "Therefore, if you are part of a typical American family, your household has about $483,000 in debt you probably don't know about." Shocked silence.

"Maybe you have a mortgage on your house," I would continue. "Well, your share of the national IOU is like a huge second or possibly third mortgage, amounting to almost ten times your annual household income—and in this case you don't even have a house to show for it."

I had them hooked.

As I said, it isn't that hard to shock people with the simple facts. Most Americans I encounter simply do not realize how rapidly our national financial obligations have grown—and how far short we are of having adequate resources to deliver on our promises. Our financial condition is as important to our national security as our military strength. Yet many of us don't have a clue about how recklessly our leaders have managed America's finances—and how vulnerable you, I, and our children are as a result.

Some of the questions I get after my speeches show this basic confusion. People ask: Whom do we owe all this money to? And what does it matter that the federal government is in debt? All it has to do is print more money.

Or they ask: If the government's spending improves our lives and promotes economic growth, what does it matter if we have a deficit? The implication is that only a heartless number cruncher—like me, by inference—would work to balance the books by cutting back on government benefits such as Social Security and Medicare.

These are all good questions, especially given how little attention our fiscal health gets in the national conversation. A fiscal crisis doesn't shoot at us. It doesn't stalk our children like a human predator. Nobody has sent each of us a bill for $483,000, and nobody will. No, the enemy I am writing about is quiet, patient, and insidious. It's a danger to our lives right now, but it's an even bigger threat to our future.

We Americans are rightly proud of the idea of the American Dream, that if we work hard and persevere, we will succeed. Each generation takes pride in passing on a better life to the next. But we need to be aware of another possibility, a nightmare in which our nation's growing financial burdens sap our society of the resources we need to maintain our economic, educational, and scientific leadership, to pay for the benefits our less-well-off citizens need, to invest in our children's future, and to maintain our unparalleled influence in the world.

How could some red numbers at the bottom of an income statement or balance sheet actually cause so much damage? Stay with me and I'll show you. I'll start by explaining the key facts of our great fiscal challenge. The goal here is to clear up some of the fog that comes from intentional obfuscation by politicians, as well as just the understandable complexity of a $14 trillion economy.

In essence, the topic of this book is very simple. It's all about how our government collects money, mainly through taxes, and spends it in government operations, programs, and benefits. These decisions on taxing and spending are called fiscal policy, and fiscal policy is all about managing our nation's finances properly. What I'm telling you in this book is that our government has been making these decisions very badly and that we have to get our fiscal house in order. If we don't, the consequences will be grave for us and for our country. But I'll do more than tell you our policies are bad. I'll give you commonsense ideas—solutions from the sensible center—to correct them.

OUR FINANCIAL HOLE

Right now, things don't look so good. Over the past several decades or so, Washington's fiscal policies have put us in that $56 trillion hole I evoke to get my audiences' attention. A lot of bad policies and practices went into creating that hole, and it's worth understanding the worst of them.

First, there's our growing budget deficit. The federal budget is Washington's annual spending list, proposed by the president, then amended and adopted by Congress. In theory it's no different from your household budget. You take account of your spendable income and make sure that your expenses don't exceed it. You borrow for big-ticket items such as a house and car, but you make sure your loan payments fit comfortably within your budget. If your spending gets too high, you had better find a way to bring in more income or you're in trouble.

All of this seems pretty obvious. But not in Washington, where the policy-making establishment often pays little attention to the difference between spending and having the money you need to pay for that spending. Most recently, the coincidence of prosperity and fiscal discipline that produced a balanced federal budget under President Clinton exploded into red ink under his successor, President Bush 43, and continues to explode under President Obama. According to the Office of Management and Budget (OMB), the federal deficit grew from $161 billion in fiscal year 2007 (a fiscal year is measured from October 1 to September 30) to $455 billion in fiscal 2008. The OMB announced in October 2009 that the federal budget deficit in fiscal 2009 was $1.42 trillion, or about 9.9 percent of GDP.

Think about that word, "trillion," if you can. The $1.42 trillion deficit translates to about $2.6 million of debt accumulated each minute, $160 million an hour, and $3.8 billion a day. Think Warren Buffett is rich? His estimated net worth is only about 2.6 percent of that $1.42 trillion.

So we should all write to our congressional representatives and demand that they cut spending enough to balance the budget, right? If only it were that simple. The budget covers two basic kinds of programs. The first are discretionary—that is, the government has full discretion as to whether to fund them and how much to give them. These include all the things that we regard as fundamental when we think about government's role: national security, homeland defense, protecting the environment, building roads, administering justice, circulating money, and so on.

Then there's the other kind of spending in our budget, called mandatory. That's right: The government has no direct control over this spending, because our elected representatives have passed laws guaranteeing benefits to people who qualify for them—such as Social Security, Medicare, and Medicaid. It's either pay the benefits or change the law, and you won't find many politicians with the courage to call for new laws to cut our Social Security, Medicare, or Medicaid costs down to size.

I think you know what's coming next. Here's a quiz: Which budget items soak up most of our government spending: (a) the discretionary programs, or (b) the mandatory programs?

The answer is, the mandatory benefit programs. They took up more than 60 percent of the $3 trillion federal budget for 2008. That means more than $1.8 trillion a year flowed from Washington on autopilot, essentially out of the government's control.

Now, how close do we come to collecting the money we need to pay for this combination of discretionary programs and mandatory spending? You know the answer to that one, too. I've already cited our $1.42 trillion budget shortfall, and this will result in more debt. But our government owes a lot of money in addition to the amounts resulting from this year's budget. It has long-term commitments to federal civilian and military retirees and to various building leases and maintenance, among other things. It also owes money to various trust funds, including the ones supporting Social Security (more on that scam later in the book). And the federal government has trillions of commitments and guarantees in response to the recent financial crisis.

Most significant, it owes money to all the domestic and foreign investors who purchased U.S. Treasury bonds in order to finance our past deficits. When you buy a Treasury bond, you are essentially lending that money to the federal government. The government must pay you back—with interest.

These obligations add to the nation's total federal debt, which includes debt held by the public (domestic and foreign investors) and debt held by the trust funds (primarily for Social Security and Medicare). That federal debt almost doubled during Bush 43's presidency and has kept on growing. As of September 30, 2009, total federal debt stood at more than $11.9 trillion. Based on the projected deficits and Social Security operations in President Obama's fiscal 2010 budget proposal and longer-range outlook, our total federal debt could double again during the next eight to ten years if we don't change our fiscal course soon.

Add debt held by the public to other liabilities—like pensions, retiree health care, and leases—and you get $12.2 trillion in total federal liabilities as of September 30, 2008. Then there are other commitments and contingencies that bring the total to $13.5 trillion. That's a lot, right?

Brace yourself. That's not the half of it. Remember those mandatory payments to Americans qualifying for government benefits of one kind or another? Well, those payments will go higher and higher as the baby boomers retire, and guess what? They haven't been funded to account for this demographic reality. We have promised trillions and trillions to recipients of Social Security, Medicare, and other programs, but we are collecting nowhere near enough in taxes and other revenues to pay what we will owe.

The idea of measuring these so-called unfunded obligations is relatively new in government accounting—probably because the number is so scary that nobody wanted to know it. It's the "don't ask, don't tell" fiscal policy. Well, here it is: Our government's unfunded obligations as of September 30, 2008, totaled approximately $42.9 trillion. Take the $13.5 trillion figure from above and add the $42.9 trillion in unfunded obligations and you have that $56 trillion hole that's been reducing my audiences to shocked silence—in fact, it was $56.4 trillion as of September 30, 2008.

And that hole is continuing to get deeper. The $56.4 trillion in total liabilities and unfunded promises as of September 30, 2008, is almost three times what it was in 2000. As I write this, the number as of September 30, 2009, is expected to be at least $63 trillion, and it is rising every second of every day—on autopilot. Why? Because of interest costs and the fact that the unfunded obligations for the Social Security and Medicare programs get worse with the passage of time.

It's almost impossible to come to terms with an obligation that big. "If you spent a million dollars a day going back to the birth of Christ," Representative Darrell E. Issa (R) of California suggested in *The New York Times* (in another context), "that wouldn't even come close to just one trillion dollars."

The unreality of the numbers lends a kind of unreality to the crisis. As the questioners in my audiences ask, whom exactly do we owe this money to? And what happens if we don't pay it? Nobody is going to lock the president and Congress into a debtors' prison. The short answer is that these obligations are real. We owe the money to Americans who expect to receive promised social benefits, Americans who work for our government and military, and Americans and foreigners who invest in Treasury bonds. Nobody's going to end up in a debtors' prison. But I will try to convince you in this book that unless we come to terms with these obligations, we will pass them on to the next generation, condemning our children to be the first Americans to face a bleaker future than their parents did.

Why can't our government cover all these obligations simply by printing more money? The short answer is that it would cheapen the U.S. dollar, weaken America's standing in the world, and touch off the kind of dramatic inflation we haven't seen in this country since the oil shocks of the 1970s—issues that I will analyze in later chapters. And don't forget, inflation is the cruelest tax of all, because you have no control over it and yet it reduces your effective purchasing power. The combined Medicare, Medicaid, and Social Security programs are growing faster than inflation.

We know what happens to countries that let their fiscal problems get out of control. I began writing this book in December 2008, on a sightseeing trip to Antarctica by way of several South American ports of call. While other passengers were worrying about icebergs, I was chilled by the ghosts of badly handled budgets past.

We stopped for a day in Buenos Aires. Argentina has been one of the most prosperous nations in Latin America, yet it has never achieved its share of economic power or influence. It has already gone bankrupt once and appeared to be heading toward its second bankruptcy. Argentineans seemed to shrug about this, as if they had no control over their fiscal disaster. I was told of an Argentine saying: "A dollar borrowed is a dollar earned." You may find yourself shaking your head at this lack of financial discipline, but the fact is that on a national level, at least, we're just as irresponsible.

HOW WE GOT HERE

In important ways, our government's fiscal policy reflects our own attitudes as citizens. Americans will never fall in love with high taxes, nor should they. The era of the tax revolt gathered steam under President Reagan in the 1980s, when we began to cut taxes and increase spending almost as a matter of political theology. That persistent antigovernment, antitax strain in our national character threatens to keep total revenues from rising high enough to match our spending.

And our spending habits, beginning in these same years, got out of control. After feasting on easy credit for so long, a culture of debt replaced the traditional American culture of thrift. Our political representatives, rather than moderating our excesses, encouraged them with low taxes and generous government benefits. Political gamesmanship replaced sound policy making. The lack of long-range planning built into our governmental system contributed to the excesses.

We all know how these excesses came to a head. The 2008–09 financial crisis, which sent our economy plummeting into recession, came after the bursting of a massive housing bubble. In the boom years leading up to that bust, big lenders got fat on profits from issuing mortgages to "subprime" borrowers—that is, to people who couldn't afford them. When the borrowers predictably de-

faulted, destroying all the exotic securities based on those mortgages, we received a terrifying lesson on the dangers of excess
debt. Did policy makers in Washington learn that lesson?

It doesn't seem so far that they have. There are disturbing parallels between the strategies followed by the financial corporations
that either crashed or required bailouts in the subprime crisis and
the way our government has been behaving in recent years. Let's
look at four of them.

First, consider the dangerous disconnect between those who
benefit from various imprudent practices and those who bear the
risk and ultimately pay the price.

In the subprime mortgage crisis, many of those who sold unsound mortgages and earned the related "origination fees" did not
hold either the mortgages or the mortgage-backed securities. Now
those who lost their homes and those who held the mortgages or
securities are paying the price—and so are taxpayers.

Is that practice so different from that of the politicians who
have increased spending, expanded government social programs,
and cut taxes without considering the long-term costs of these actions? After all, today's taxpayers benefit from low-tax and high-
spend policies, and tomorrow's taxpayers will pay the price for
today's irresponsible behavior.

Second, remember how impenetrably complicated the subprime shenanigans were? They were hard to explain to anybody
on the outside—and obviously to many inside players as well.

Many of the securitized mortgage products and related "insurance" arrangements were very complex, and there was not enough
transparency about their size, nature, and related risks. In some
cases, banks and other financial institutions created off-the-books
entities so that regulators and others would find it hard to trace the
risks to the firms' health. As a result, when things hit the fan, many
investors and regulators alike suffered big, bad surprises.

Is that so different from the way the U.S. government handles its finances? For example, the annual federal budget deficits are understated because they figure in a Social Security surplus that actually exists only on paper. As I will explain in the Social Security chapter, that surplus was credited to so-called trust funds, but the cash actually was spent and replaced with U.S. IOU bonds. They are not readily marketable, but the government is obligated to repay them— with interest. Got that? The financial geniuses who are expert at muddying up corporate finances with complex, off-balance-sheet transactions don't have much on the budget magicians of our government.

Third, note that many of the corporations crippled by the subprime crisis conducted their mad dash for profits while paying too little attention to the danger signs, including mounting debt, dwindling cash flow, and unrealistic credit ratings.

It's pretty obvious that corporations and individuals took on too much debt as they sought the false gains of the housing bubble. It's also clear that corporations and individuals didn't focus enough on whether their cash flows were adequate to cover their obligations. Too many investors trusted a Triple-A credit rating—a judgment by one or more of the credit-rating agencies—even when it told them that a major corporation awash in complex mortgage derivatives actually was in great shape. Not surprisingly, when the bubble burst, some of what the agencies had rated as gold immediately turned to junk.

Is that so different from our federal government's cavalier attitude toward debt? Washington is adding debt at record rates and becoming increasingly reliant on foreign lenders. To put things in perspective, we took on debt equal to only 40 percent of our economy to win our independence as a nation and to gain agreement on the U.S. Constitution. At the end of World War II, while we had debt equal to 122 percent of our economy, we had virtually no foreign debt.

Look at where we are today. As of September 30, 2009, we

were expected to have total debt equal to approximately 85 percent of our economy, and that was expected to approach 95 percent by the end of fiscal 2010. After that, our debt levels are expected to skyrocket absent dramatic reforms. (See figure 1. If this doesn't get your attention, I am not sure what will.) And today, about half of our nation's public debt is held by foreign lenders, up from about 19 percent in 1990 and essentially zero after World War II, and that percentage is on the rise. The major credit rating agencies still are giving the United States a Triple-A rating. But they have noted that this rating is "at risk" if we don't start putting our financial house in order soon. China and other foreign lenders have also expressed their concern in various public statements and private actions.

In addition to mounting public debt, the Medicare and Social Security disability programs are already in a negative cash-flow position. The Social Security retirement and survivors income pro-

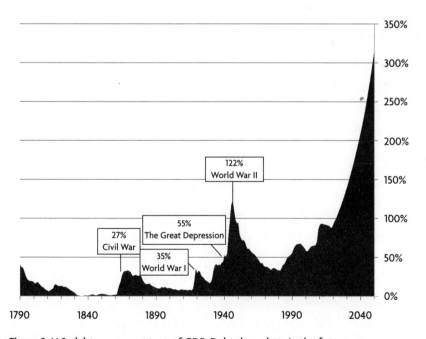

Figure 1 U.S. debt as a percentage of GDP: Debt skyrockets in the future.

gram is now expected to join them in 2010. That is not good news, because cash flow is key.

Fourth, recall how neither the major corporations nor our government addressed the growing risks of the housing bubble until it had burst into a full-blown crisis.

Corporate risk managers failed to adequately anticipate the disaster scenario for housing prices. Corporate overseers, including boards of directors, did not do an adequate job of monitoring related risks.

Is that so different from the government's lax vigilance? The deregulation in the late 1990s allowed financial service companies to engage in a broader range of activities and take on a greater level of risk. This expansion was not coupled with adequate corporate and federal transparency, accountability, and oversight. Simply put, federal regulators allowed too many players on the field and too few referees. Former Federal Reserve chairman Alan Greenspan has noted in retrospect that he assumed that corporate managers would serve as their own referees, effectively mitigating the related risks. He was wrong, and he has admitted that.

In the final analysis, greed won out over prudence, and we are still suffering the consequences. Let's be sure that our federal government's finances don't reach that level of crisis. After all, the stakes and risks are much greater for both America and the world.

THE SCARY BUDGET NUMBERS

The recession and attendant financial shock appear to be easing as I write this. But in Washington, financial imprudence is part of the fabric of government. You can see that in a single document that gets updated every year: the U.S. budget. In putting together the budget, the president and Congress set our national priorities and allocate resources among them. The results have been pretty consistent. Over the forty years ending in 2008, revenues have averaged about 18.3 percent of our economy and spending has averaged over 20.6 percent, resulting in an average deficit of about 2.4 percent.

But that gap began to widen under Bush 43, who cut taxes while starting two wars, bolstering homeland security, adding an expensive prescription drug benefit to Medicare, and increasing other spending. In 2007, the federal deficit stood at $161 billion, or 1.2 percent of our economy. In 2008 it was $455 billion, or 3.2 percent. In 2009, figuring in the billions spent to pull our economy out of recession and on various bailout efforts, the deficit rocketed to about $1.42 trillion, 9.9 percent of our economy.

In Washington, they speak of our "fiscal exposure"—the sum of all the benefits, programs, debt payments, and other expenses that will cost us big bucks in the future whether or not we want to cut spending. The term I've used for all of that is our "federal financial hole." In the first eight years of this century it has grown from $20.4 trillion to $56.4 trillion—a 176 percent increase. Maybe you have a few bills—mortgage payment, auto loan, cable TV, phone—deducted automatically from your checking account. How would you feel if those expenses had risen 176 percent in eight years while your income remained steady?

The hole is getting deeper because we are doing little to bring our income into line with our spending. And until now I haven't even talked about the interest payments on our federal debt. Suppose our government fails to increase federal revenues above the current rate. Based on the GAO's latest long-range alternative budget simulation, within about twelve years, our interest payments will become the largest single expenditure in the federal budget. By 2040, all of our federal tax revenues will add up to enough to cover only our two biggest expenses: interest on our debt and Medicare and Medicaid. Everything else—Social Security, defense, education, road building, you name it—will fail to be funded.

As you know, benefits payments are the biggest chunk of the

government's massive obligation. Since the 1960s, the growth of these mandatory payments has overtaken what we spend on defense as a share of our national output—and what we spend on everything else in our federal budget, from law enforcement to border protection, children's programs to national parks, highways to foreign aid.

Although defense has declined dramatically as a percentage of the overall federal budget over the past forty years, we have actually increased total defense spending. In recent years, we have added resources to fight terrorism abroad. That means that other discretionary programs are much more susceptible to cutting. These include education, research, transportation, infrastructure, and other programs that, if properly designed and effectively executed, can promote economic growth and development. How will squeezing those areas serve to keep America great?

All of this puts us in a major-league quandary. Our nation has to bring what we earn into line with what we spend at a time when our spending literally is out of control. One option—cutting investments in America's future in order to finance our large and growing mandatory spending programs—is another way of cheating the next generation. Unfortunately, today we are both cutting our investments in the future and handing our descendants a mountain of debt. That is a double whammy for young people and the unborn. It's not just irresponsible, it's immoral and downright un-American. More on that later.

Two

AMERICA 2030: WHY WE MUST ACT—NOW

Those of you who are parents (and I'm a parent) may want to reject out of hand the idea that we are in effect stealing from our children's future and bequeathing to them a far less prosperous life. But if we don't begin to address our fiscal challenges soon, it's only a matter of time before the consequences begin to show up, most likely starting with higher interest rates. As things get worse, our children will slowly see their living standards decline. We can still prevent these things from happening. The ultimate goal of cleaning up our fiscal policy is not to avoid a recession or even to balance the budget per se—it's to pass on the kind of healthy, vibrant nation that we inherited.

It's easy to fall back on generalities—that America is a great country, and that we always rise to great challenges and will do so again. True, but we can only succeed by taking action, and we have a lot of action to take. Let's say we do take only small steps to address our fiscal crisis. Let's say we stop cutting taxes, but we don't increase them radically either. Let's say our government continues to take in about the same level of historical revenues, but we hold discretionary spending to 2008 levels as a percentage of the economy, and we don't expand health care or other entitlements any further. That sounds pretty benign, but it's actually a disaster scenario for our children.

Let's take the example of kids born in early 2000, when our national budget was in balance and the technology-powered future seemed bright.

During the first eight years of their lives, we have learned, the nation's financial hole grew by 176 percent to $56.4 trillion. And the number is not standing still. That was its size as of September 30, 2008—before the official declaration of a recession, before the significant market declines of October 2008, and before the big stimulus and bailout bills designed to jump-start the economy and address our immediate financial crisis. In fiscal 2007, recall, our budget deficit was $161 billion, or 1.2 percent of the economy. By 2009, the deficit soared to $1.42 trillion, which is about 9.9 percent of the economy. Just think about that for a second. Our federal deficit grew by almost nine times in the past two fiscal years!

Given our scenario—no benefit cuts, no tax hikes—the government would have to finance this gaping hole mainly by borrowing money from domestic and foreign investors, with interest. Don't forget, according to the GAO's latest long-range budget simulation, even without an increase in overall interest rates, our interest payments would become the largest single expenditure in the federal budget in about twelve years. And what do we get for that interest? Nothing!

Of course, something will have to give before we get to that point. However, the government has overpromised and underdelivered for far too long. How can we fix things? Will we cut benefits, those mandatory payments that are chiseled into law? Or will we raise taxes to onerous levels? We will probably have to do some combination of both. That is, we will have to renegotiate the social contract with our fellow citizens and raise taxes. However we do that, our kids will pay the price. And the bigger the bill we pass on to them, the bleaker the future we will bequeath to them.

Let's assume that Washington policy makers continue to punt on making tough spending choices and ultimately raise taxes to address the growing deficits. Nobody will reach in our kids' pockets and take their money because the government will take it before it even reaches their pockets. What will that mean for their after-tax income? Right now, on average, Americans pay about 21 percent of their income in federal taxes and another 10 percent to state and local governments. By 2030, to pay our rising bills, that amount could be at least 45 percent—higher even than the average 42 percent that most Europeans pay. By 2040, it would be at least 53 percent and climbing. In reality, total taxes in 2030 and 2040 would be even higher than these estimates because of the fiscal challenges facing state and local governments—such as Medicaid costs, unfunded retiree health care promises, underfunded pension plans, deferred maintenance and other critical infrastructure needs, and higher education funding.

With reductions in disposable income like that, the children of 2000 will inherit a much different kind of America in 2030. That's when they will be turning thirty, entering their most productive years.

So much of their money will be devoted to keeping the government afloat that they'll have relatively little for everything else in life. Their homes will be smaller and drabber. There will be less to spend for cars, vacations, dinners out, and big TV sets, all of which their parents took for granted. They'll still read about the consumer society and conspicuous consumption, but mainly in history texts. Maybe it's a good idea for America to become less materialistic—but the idea should be to give our children that choice, not to impoverish them.

The resulting financial pressures will take a toll on the young families of 2030. Financial problems are the number one cause of divorce and family tensions—and there will be a lot more of those.

The collective loss of spending power will likely cost our country in broader ways. Our young families in 2030 may conclude that a third or even second child is beyond their means. Right now Americans have a birthrate of 2.1 children per family. That is, we are replacing ourselves, which gives us an advantage over other industrial countries like Japan and Russia, where the birthrate is falling. But that advantage may not last if the next generation of American parents simply can't afford to have that many kids.

Think of these young adults of 2030 looking at the generations that come before and after them. They will have less to offer their children, including fewer educational opportunities. They will still have some version of Social Security and Medicare, but much of their hard-earned money will have gone to pay the nation's debts— leaving them with nothing like the retirements of prosperity and travel that the boomers are about to enjoy.

These young adults of 2030 are alive right now. They are my grandchildren, and I am embarrassed by the mess we are passing on to them. If I were a young American looking at this kind of future, I wouldn't exactly be saying, "Thanks, folks." I would be marching out in front of the nation's capitol waving a sign that protested taxation without representation.

When my youngest granddaughter, Grace, was three years old, I told her about what the federal government was doing to her future. Believe it or not, her response was, "Devastating, Granddaddy." If a three-year-old can get it (and how about that vocabulary?), Washington ought to get it.

Young people won't be the only ones affected. What would you do if the government took twice as much of your income out of your paycheck? Could you afford to take a nice vacation? Would you have to get rid of your second car? Would you have to move to a smaller house? Could you afford to send your kids to college? Would you be able to have the retirement lifestyle that you always dreamed of? If you think it's tough today, you ain't seen nothing yet based on our current path.

While these consequences are bad enough, much higher interest rates and inflation levels would likely precede any dramatic tax increases. Higher interest rates result in tighter credit and higher effective costs for anything that requires a loan. Inflation is nothing but destructive, robbing us of our incomes and savings. Contrary to assertions by some people, we can't grow or inflate our way out of our fiscal challenge. Why? Because the math doesn't come close to working. Inflation reduces our purchasing power no matter what our income level is.

THE COST TO OUR NATIONAL STANDING

More than our families and lifestyle are at stake. Our fiscal imbalance at home can damage America's overall economic strength and our leadership in the world. Global diplomacy is the ultimate stage for realpolitik. If you are weak economically, you are weak in every other way, and your influence declines. If you have less money to invest in education, in scientific research, in critical infrastructure, your national well-being will suffer—and so will your national competitiveness.

Our fiscal weakness already makes us uncomfortably reliant on others. Here's how. In the past few years, you and I have been able to shop till we drop because interest rates have been so low, making money cheap.

Why has the cost of credit been so low? In part because in China and other countries people have accumulated a lot of American dollars from the exports they sell us and save a lot more than we do. They need to do something with that money, so they often invest in American Treasury bonds. The huge demand for our bonds has helped our government issue them at low interest rates. That, in turn, helps to keep our interest rates low and credit available. For a long time, that cheap credit kept housing values high (if your mortgage rate is low, you can afford a more expensive home), thereby giving Americans leverage to buy more.

There is a price to be paid for being unduly dependent on foreign lenders. To a significant extent, we are putting our economic health in their hands. The U.S. government has gone from having no foreign debt right after World War II to about 19 percent of public debt in 1990 to about 50 percent as of August 2009, and the level is still climbing. (See figure 2.) In short, America is being mortgaged. And increasingly that mortgage is being held by non-Americans. Among our top lenders are countries whose national interests can diverge from our own, including China, Russia, and oil giants like Venezuela, Saudi Arabia, Nigeria, and Iran.

This dangerous dependence on foreign lenders is not in our nation's economic, diplomatic, or national security interests, nor does it support our domestic tranquility over the long term. For

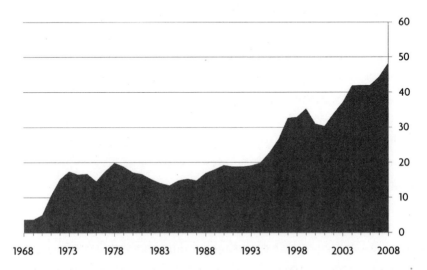

Figure 2 Percentage of U.S. public debt held by foreign lenders. America's reliance on foreign lenders has grown dramatically, passing 50 percent in 2009.

one thing, we are vulnerable to policy changes by our investors. What if a huge partner like China decides to cultivate its domestic market to a greater extent, requiring it to buy fewer U.S. bonds? That could well cause U.S. interest rates to rise, making it more expensive for us to buy everything from autos to real estate.

We also have to worry about angering our key investors. We can't play hardball with China on human rights or dispute its claims to Taiwan at a time when Beijing is our biggest lender. Let's get real. China is not going to lend us money to defend Taiwan. After all, national pride is more important than money.

Investors from abroad have begun to flex their muscles. To satisfy the concerns of China, among other reasons, the U.S. Treasury said in the summer of 2009 that it would issue greater quantities of bonds that pay a dividend higher than any change in the consumer price index. That's a hedge against inflation. The demand for more U.S. inflation-protected bonds demonstrates China's worries that America's massive borrowing and spending, combined with the Federal Reserve's loose monetary policy, will ignite a damaging round of inflation once the economy turns around.

Our foreign lenders have already shown that they are ready to use their leverage to get what they want. Consider the debt issued by Fannie Mae and Freddie Mac, companies sponsored by the U.S. government to stimulate the mortgage market. Although both enterprises functioned as private corporations, they had a public purpose and had a number of political figures on their boards.

As a result, many foreign investors assumed that the U.S. government guaranteed these corporations' debt, even though U.S. law did not provide for any such guarantee. When Fannie Mae and Freddie Mac got into trouble, these foreign investors, especially the Japanese and Chinese—our nation's largest lenders— demanded that the U.S. government guarantee them. Washington complied. That's why we taxpayers now stand behind more than $5 trillion in Fannie Mae and Freddie Mac debt obligations in order to protect foreign investors. It is too soon to say what our ultimate cost will be, but now we know that federal officials have to pay attention to what our foreign lenders say.

Let's see how willingly the foreigners pour in the money when we run trillion-dollar-plus deficits several years in a row, or after our baby boomers stop working and start drawing on the retirement and health benefits we have promised them. That huge social shift will put enormous new pressure on America's finances and may give these lenders second thoughts about how much more money to lend us and at what rate of interest.

There is no way we can increase our workforce fast enough to keep up with that kind of obligation. As we look to the future, fewer workers will support a growing number of retirees. This will place an increasingly unfair burden on younger workers, who will end up bearing the brunt of future tax increases needed to finance the federal government's programs and promises.

The recent financial crisis and recession do have one bright side. Americans are beginning to understand the consequences of taking on too much debt. (I certainly hope this book helps spread the word!) And yes, many Americans for the first time in their lives now know what a "rainy day" looks like. As a result, many are starting to be more cautious about their spending and their use of credit. They are also starting to save more. This may slow economic growth in the short term, but it will help us to achieve more sustainable growth over time.

At the start of this chapter, I wrote about the dangers of a do-nothing policy and called that a disaster scenario, crippling the future of our children and of our nation. But actually, what I have written so far is not the worst-case scenario. It assumes that we will eventually work our way out of the present financial crisis, avoid reaching the tipping point of confidence in our ability to put our federal financial house in order, and keep our society together.

President Obama has taken steps to get the economy moving

and to restore public confidence. The price tag has been high, and the "cure" will add greatly to our national debt load. What if our federal financial hole keeps getting deeper? There will come a time when the foreign lenders who have been propping up our prosperity will stop believing in the strength of our financial system. It's true that China, Japan, and certain other countries can't call our debt and have reason to want us to continue to buy their exports. However, what if these foreign lenders lost confidence in America's ability to put its financial house in order and took much of their money elsewhere? That's when you could expect real trouble. We would start talking about a dramatic decline in the value of the dollar combined with a dramatic increase in interest rates, all of which could lead to a new Great Depression—a true worst-case scenario.

We need more than Obama's economic rescue plan. We need a national fiscal recovery plan, a way to fundamentally transform how our government collects and spends our money. It must be based on principled, systemic reforms that lead us toward a new era of responsible spending that is consonant with American values and our obligations to the next generation. Let's explore those principles and values in the next chapter.

Three

PRINCIPLES FROM OUR HISTORY AND COMMON SENSE

I have traveled to more than forty-five states and met with many thousands of people since September 2005. I always bring along my charts and graphs on deficit and debt trends and my projections showing how they are set to skyrocket in the future. I also explain our increasing foreign dependency and the deepening federal financial hole. All of these get my audiences' attention. But do you know what really captures their imagination? When I remind them that we are all Americans, and I ask them to think of our fiscal crisis in terms of the principles and values that we all learned at home and in grade school. And do you know what tugs at their hearts? It's when I show them a picture of my three grandchildren and talk about my concern for their future.

We've all heard about our founding principles and values a million times: Americans believe in individual rights and equal opportunity, as well as the personal responsibilities that come with them. We support freedom, democracy, and our Constitution. That Constitution claims its authority based on the will of "We the People" but at the same time makes clear that the government it creates has limited powers. For our Founding Fathers, the aim of government was not only to provide order and security, but also to preserve human liberty. Anyone on the ideological spectrum from the far right to the far left should be able to agree with those basic principles. That's why the Founding Fathers offer us a useful starting point in our efforts to transform ourselves and our federal government.

I take these founding principles seriously, as someone whose family came to America in the 1680s. The plain truth is that over the years we have strayed from many of them. Now we must come back to this bedrock. Like any prudent exercise in political decision making, a sound fiscal policy should reflect our basic principles and values, since they define who we are as a society. If you look at our fiscal policies from this perspective, we come off looking not just irresponsible but downright un-American. Let's examine how.

The Founding Fathers created a government empowered to achieve a set of general goals for the new nation, while at the same time separating and limiting the powers of that government. The broad goals—"to form a more perfect Union, establish Justice, insure domestic Tranquility, provide for the common defence, promote the general Welfare, and secure the Blessings of Liberty"—are laid out in the preamble to the Constitution. Fearful of concentrations of power in any agency of government, they separated those powers among the Congress, the executive branch, and the federal judiciary. And, in a delicate balancing act, they sought to energize the new government by granting to the Congress important new powers—including the authority to levy and collect taxes, to borrow money, to regulate commerce with foreign nations and among the states, and to declare war.

In fact, during its early years of operation, the new federal government used these powers sparingly. The government used its powers of taxation to pay off the substantial debt of the Revolutionary War. Aside from that obligation, however, the principal expense of government involved running a postal service and overseeing the collection of customs duties.

Look where we are now. In fiscal 2008, you could trace less than 40 percent of our federal government spending back to the bedrock responsibilities envisioned by the founders. In budget language, all of those original programs and the others that relate to the responsibilities reserved to the federal government under the Constitution, including national defense, foreign relations, and the federal judicial system, are considered discretionary.

Early Americans gave us not only òur love of individual rights and responsibilities but the economic manifestations of those principles. Their culture valued thrift and savings and frowned on debt. While America's farmers of the Revolutionary years bought their land and financed their operations on a web of credit, excessive debt was abhorred, meriting time in a debtors' prison.

Today, too many Americans have followed the bad example of the modern federal government and have become addicted to debt. Those who get too deeply into hock simply file for bankruptcy. There is little to no shame in that these days. In fact, too many individuals and businesses look to bankruptcy as an acceptable exit strategy from excessive debt. Today, we no longer have debtors' prisons, and I'm not suggesting that we bring them back; however, we now have something closer to debtors' pardons, and that's not good.

The very idea of thriftiness is now as antiquated as the piggy bank. Earlier in our history, the practice of saving for the future—of taking responsibility for our own financial lives—was taken for granted. In the 1930s, President Franklin D. Roosevelt and the New Deal created social programs to help Americans ruined by financial losses from the Great Depression, including the Social Security program. At the time, Roosevelt described Social Security as a modest offer to "give some measure of protection to the average citizen and to his family against the loss of a job and against poverty-ridden old age."

Look what has happened since then. About 35 percent of Americans rely on Social Security for 90 percent or more of their retirement income. The fact is, too many Americans look to the government to secure their retirement because they don't save enough on their own. And Social Security is only one example. Over the years, the federal government has created a number of social insurance programs—including the Medicare plans for doctors' visits and prescription drugs—that provide significant taxpayer subsidies to even middle- and upper-income Americans.

We started these programs as a safety net for our hard-luck fellow citizens, and of course that safety net must remain strong. My point is that programs designed to help the needy should not become enshrined as benefits to which all are entitled. Too many of us who can afford to contribute more to our own well-being are jumping into the safety net instead. That approach is not affordable or sustainable. More important, it's not the American way.

WAR AND DIPLOMACY

The framers of our Constitution also set out various founding principles to guide our nation in its relations with other countries. True, the world has changed a lot since our founders admonished us to avoid meddling in foreign conflicts. George Washington asked: Why should we "entangle our peace and prosperity in the toils of European ambition, rival-ship, interest, humor or caprice?" The answer is that today we have no choice but to involve ourselves with others on a whole range of issues.

Today we live in a wired world that is more interconnected and interdependent than ever. Many of our imports, including oil, are critical to our economy. As a result, we sometimes must concern ourselves in the affairs of Europe, the Middle East, and elsewhere in order to ensure stability and protect our national interests. The key is to decide when it is and is not appropriate to do so. These issues deserve much more serious deliberation than they have been getting in recent years. One thing I am pretty sure of: General Washington would not have been happy with our predicament today, when our economic health is desperately dependent on the caprices of foreign lenders.

The Constitution is perfectly clear on one aspect of foreign policy. It dictates that "the Congress shall have power . . . to declare war." As the framers saw it, the business of making war was a joint responsibility of Congress and the president in his role as commander in chief. Typically, presidents ask the Congress to declare war. However, in recent years we've followed a "don't ask, don't declare" policy. What would General Washington have thought of our undeclared wars in Korea, Vietnam, the Persian Gulf, and Afghanistan? And what about our first preemptive war, in Iraq, a nation that had made no substantiated threat against us before we invaded it and overthrew its government?

When our most recent President George—Bush 43—left office, we were fighting two undeclared wars at once. By failing to declare these wars, Congress effectively abdicated its constitutional responsibility to the president. I recognize that today's world moves much more quickly than the world of the eighteenth century. Today, we have to respond immediately and decisively to sudden provocations—when terrorists attack one of our cities, for example, or when some rogue nation fires a missile at us. The president alone has the power and flexibility to defend our nation in a circumstance like that. All the same, we must not lose sight of our constitutional principles. We should never invade a sovereign nation, committing our blood and wealth, unless Congress has declared war.

Why is that important in a book about fiscal policy? By failing to seek or consider a declaration of war, Congress and the president avoided important debates of the related costs, benefits, and consequences. Furthermore, Congress put itself in the untenable position of having to fund the conflicts as long as the president wants to keep troops in the field. Once you ask our military to risk life and limb, you must fund our forces even if there is no exit strategy and no clear end point; for example, the surrender of the country you declared war against.

Americans were not rallied to support the wars in Afghanistan and Iraq, nor were we asked to pay for them properly through bond purchases and higher taxes. A more thorough process would have forced us to think hard about the potential costs and consequences and to help engender more public understanding and support once a decision was made. Commitments like these would have united us behind these causes—and, not incidentally, led us to pay for them responsibly. Americans should contribute directly and proudly to our war efforts. Once Congress declares a war, all of us should join the effort to win it.

BIG GOVERNMENT, LOW TAXES

Washington today no longer seems to work for "We the People." Our founders sought to banish the elaborate European-style privilege and bureaucracy that they had escaped. While their experience had taught them to be on guard against corruption in politics, they nevertheless regarded engagement in politics as a high calling—as an opportunity to serve the public interest. Men such as George Washington, John Adams, Thomas Jefferson, and Benjamin Franklin lived in an age when it was possible to pursue politics not as a full-time profession, but as a form of civic obligation, a natural extension of their occupational roles as farmers, lawyers, or businessmen.

Today's professional politicians, as we often lament, are cut from entirely different cloth. While there are a number of dedicated and capable elected officials, too many current members of the U.S. Senate and House have grown out of touch with the real world through long careers in the federal government. If and when they do decide to leave office, many move into high-paying jobs as corporate or special-interest lobbyists in Washington. As a result, too few work for us; they work to advance their own careers. Yes, there are exceptions to this rule on both sides of the political aisle, but they are dwindling in number and influence. Some of the biggest exceptions who are fighting for more federal fiscal responsibility are Senators Conrad (D-ND), Gregg (R-NH), Lieberman (Ind.-CT), and Voinovich (R-OH), along with House members Hoyer (D-MD), Cooper (D-TN) and Wolf (R-VA). Former Senator Pete Dominici (R-NM) and others have also joined the fight.

What about personal ethics and public morality? The founders of our nation were acutely aware of the way in which posterity might judge them. While they had no desire for celebrity, they all aspired to achieve fame, which, in their lexicon, was synonymous with honor. It was this striving for "lofty ambition," to use the phrase of the French traveler Alexis de Tocqueville, that sometimes caused America's leaders to go to extremes. One of the most ambitious of our Founding Fathers, Alexander Hamilton, was also one of the most obsessed with honor, an obsession that would cost him his life in his duel with Aaron Burr. Today's political leaders are perhaps too often seduced by another, less lofty, kind of ambition—the striving for power and personal influence for its own sake, not for the larger good of the society which they are charged with serving.

No wonder many Americans have lost their hope and optimism for our nation. For the first time in our history, a majority of Americans believe that life for their children will not be better than their own. Why? In large part because in addition to straying from what made this nation great, America faces a range of large and growing challenges to our way of life that Washington policy makers are largely ignoring. America faces a serious leadership deficit—a problem we certainly didn't have at the birth of our republic. That is our most serious deficit of all. How did we lose our way?

I don't have to tell you that this is no longer the America of 1789. We have made great progress on some imposing issues, such as civil rights and equal justice. But we have lost our way in developing the idea at the root of American political thinking in the early days—limited government. Since those days, our expectations have gotten more expansive. Over the decades, the growth of the government's role in our lives came in response to real needs dictated by our development, including periodic economic crises. As we have learned over the years, measures adopted during a crisis can sometimes last indefinitely. The same can be said for public programs and tax policies that have outlived their usefulness or just don't generate real results.

That historical trend has left us with a big government that is constantly at war with a philosophy of personal responsibility and individual liberty that demands a limited government. We have created big-government programs, but we try to finance them with small-government taxes. That spells deficits and debt, and if we don't reconcile these conflicting views of government, it will spell insolvency for the government and a worse life for many Americans. We have to balance our ideas about what government can do with our recognition of what it should do and what we are willing to pay for.

A number of presidents had good reason for expanding the scope of government and ramping up federal spending. Franklin Roosevelt created Social Security and the other New Deal programs to help lift us out of the Great Depression. Lyndon Johnson created Medicare and built his Great Society to combat festering poverty and racial injustices. Social-welfare spending increased even more under Richard Nixon, who fought to put out the fires in America's cities at a time of riots, unrest, and the Vietnam War. Ronald Reagan built up our defenses in his climactic battle against the "evil" Soviet empire. And Bush 43 launched two wars and bolstered our homeland defenses for the struggle against terrorism.

For most of our history, even as the role of government grew, our nation took pride in being fiscally prudent. We did not run large deficits and accumulate significant debt burdens without a clear and compelling national reason. That record lasted until the 1980s, when Americans began to see deficits and debt as acceptable, although not desirable. Some of our presidents fought this trend. Bush 41 and Clinton both broke campaign promises, cut spending, raised taxes, and imposed tough statutory budget controls. While they both paid a political price for their actions, they deserve great credit for having the courage to act in the best interest of the country. They did what was right rather than what was popular. That is what true leadership is all about.

The statutory budget controls that were imposed in the 1990s remained in place until the end of fiscal 2002. They included, among other things, caps on discretionary spending increases, and requirements that any new spending or tax cuts be paid for within a ten-year period. (These were called the pay-as-you-go, or PAYGO, rules.) The statutory controls helped to take our country from large and growing deficits to large and growing surpluses. They also provided a basis for elected officials to say no to requests from constituents and special interest groups.

Once PAYGO expired, however, Washington lost control. Bush 43's serial tax cuts, on top of his greatly increased spending, destroyed the balanced budget that Clinton had turned over to him. While we faced large and growing budget surpluses when Bush 43 entered office, we faced huge and growing deficits when he left office. (See figure 3.) In the midst of the Bush cuts, his vice president,

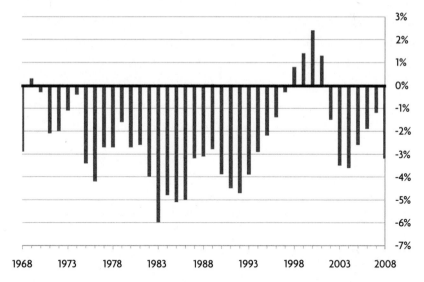

Figure 3 U.S. annual budget deficit or surplus as a percentage of GDP. The federal bottom line: The deficit trends are clear and concerning. The deficit for 2009 is about 10 percent of GDP and would not even fit in the figure above!

Dick Cheney, famously told Treasury secretary Paul O'Neill—as O'Neill recalled it—that "Ronald Reagan proved that deficits don't matter." (I believe Cheney was referring to the political cost of deficits. I certainly hope he wasn't talking about the economic cost. If he was, he was flat wrong.)

The question is, can Obama turn around this financial disaster in the making? His first budget, for fiscal 2010, contained more truth and transparency about war costs, tax provisions, and health care reimbursement rates than Bush's did. Our new president promises that his reforms, while expensive on the front end, will reduce costs and cut the deficit as time goes on. However, we have a long way to go before we can say that we are adequately disclosing and dealing with the huge sums that lie below the surface, off the balance sheet, and beyond the ten-year budget horizon used by the federal government. (Obama's early months in office will be examined more closely in the next chapter.)

Obama's predecessors also faced pressures to keep the costs of government down—but some of them failed to meet that challenge. Johnson's and Nixon's reluctance to raise taxes to finance the Vietnam War and other federal spending helped lead to "stagflation"—rising unemployment and inflation—during the 1970s. Reagan's "tax revolt"—unaccompanied by spending cuts—kick-started our nationwide addiction to deficits and debt.

WHAT THE PAST TELLS US

Perhaps because we are a young country, Americans tend not to pay much attention to the lessons of history. Well, we should start, because those lessons are brutal. Power, even great power, if not well tended, erodes over time. Nations, like corporations and people, can lose discipline and morale. Economic and political vulnerability go hand in hand. Remember, without a strong economy, a nation's international standing, standard of living, national security, and even its domestic tranquility will suffer over time.

Many of us think that a superpowerful, prosperous nation like America will be a permanent fixture dominating the world scene. We are too big to fail. But you don't have to delve far into the history books to see what has happened to other once-dominant powers. Most of us have witnessed seismic political shifts in our lifetime. In 1985, Mikhail Gorbachev settled into his job as the Soviet Union's young and charismatic new leader and began acting on his mandate to reenergize the socialist empire. Seven years later that empire collapsed and disappeared from the face of the Earth. Gorbachev runs a think tank in Moscow now.

In a sense, the larger world is starting to resemble the nasty and brutish life that long has characterized the corporate world. Just ask Jeffrey Immelt, chairman and CEO of General Electric. Of the twelve giants that made up the first Dow Jones Industrial Average in 1896—all of them once considered too big to fail—only GE remains. The other towering names of the era—the American Cotton Oil Company, the U.S. Leather Company, the Chicago Gas Company, and the like—all have faded away. And as GE stands against the winds of today's financial challenges, ask Immelt whether there is such thing as a company that is too big to fail.

I love to read history books for the lessons they offer. After all, as the homily goes, if you don't learn from history, you may be doomed to repeat it. Great powers rise and fall. None has a covenant to perpetuate itself without cost. The millennium of the Roman Empire—which included five hundred years as a republic—came to an end in the fifth century after scores of years of gradual decay. We Americans often study that Roman endgame with trepidation. We ask, as Cullen Murphy put it in the title of his provocative 2007 book, are we Rome?

The trouble is not that we see ourselves as an empire with global swagger. But we do see ourselves as a superpower with global responsibilities—guardians if not enforcers of a Pax Americana. And as a global power, America presents unsettling parallels with the disintegration of Rome—a decline of moral values, a loss of political civility, an overextended military, an inability to control national borders, and a growth of fiscal irresponsibility by the central government. Do these sound familiar?

Finally, there is what Murphy calls the "complexity parallel": Mighty powers like America and Rome grow so big and sprawling that they become impossible to manage. In comparing the two, he writes, one should "think less about the ability of a superpower to influence everything on earth, and more about how everything on earth affects a superpower."

A superpower that is financially reliant on others can be vulnerable to foreign influence. The British Empire learned this in 1956, when Britain and France were contesting control of the Suez Canal with Egypt. The Soviet Union was threatening to intervene on Egypt's side, turning the regional dispute into a global showdown between Moscow and Washington. The Eisenhower administration wanted to avoid that, and the United States also happened to control the bulk of Britain's foreign debt. President Eisenhower demanded that the British and French withdraw. When they refused, the United States quietly threatened to sell off a significant amount of its holdings in the British pound, which would have effectively destroyed Britain's currency. The British and French backed down and withdrew from Suez within weeks.

The U.S. dollar has never come under a direct foreign attack (though its vulnerability is growing). A direct foreign attack would result in a dramatic move away from the dollar. That would lead to a significant decline in its value, as well as higher interest rates. This is often referred to by economists as a "hard landing." In lay terms, it's more like a crash landing. Still, Americans have become intimately acquainted with the shocks of financial instability. Americans of a certain age still vividly recall the depths of the Depression in the 1930s and the chaos of inflation and long gasoline lines during the oil shock of the 1970s. We will also remember the financial collapse that began in 2008, and we pray for nothing worse. Some of our smartest financial thinkers are praying right along with us. "I do think that piling up more and more and more external debt and having the rest of the world own more and more of the United States may create real political instability down the line," investor Warren Buffett has said, "and increases the possibility that demagogues [will] come along and do some very foolish things."

CONNECTING PAST AND FUTURE

This is another major lesson we must take from the history books: No power is too big to fail. The greatest of nations must demonstrate again and again that it is strong, smart, and flexible enough to keep its predominance.

Our twenty-first-century economy can be our most productive and our future can be better than our past—if we return to the principles and values that made us great. In the expanded international arena, money, goods, people, and information all move freely and rapidly. Just look at where our T-shirts, technology, and cars are manufactured, and who buys our aircraft, software, and surgical systems, and you can see that we are no longer a self-contained nation. The world's growing interdependence, with all of its benefits, also challenges American policy makers to find new ways to form international partnerships to achieve our vital national goals. I don't need to tell you that financially predominant nations have more cooperative partners. Needless to say, governments that aspire to the role of global superpower are not drowning in debt.

Transformation has always been an American strength. The impulse to remake and improve our lives is woven into our national fabric. Thomas Jefferson, writing to his friend James Madison in December of 1787, confessed, "I am not a friend to a very energetic government. It is always oppressive." But even a staunch believer in limited government like Jefferson realized that governments must change with the times. Writing in 1816, after serving two terms as president and reflecting on America's rapid westward expansion and increasing involvement in the world economy, he proclaimed, "We might as well require a man to wear still the coat which fitted him when a boy, as civilized society to remain ever under the regimen of their barbarous ancestors."

As a nation, we need to follow both of Jefferson's impulses. We need to support those government programs that truly do help us achieve the core aims spelled out in the preamble of our Constitution. At the same time, we need to weed out those programs that are either ineffective or contrary to our national goals and better target some of the ones that remain. We need to be realistic about what we can afford and sustain over time. As Jefferson also said, "It is incumbent on every generation to pay its own debts as it goes." It's time for tough choices and tough love in Washington.

The societies that have survived great challenges and turmoil in their histories succeeded by reinvigorating their basic principles, returning to their core values, and reinventing their place in the world. That is how Germany and Japan recovered their national identities and their economies after World War II. That is how China is shaking off centuries of stagnation, foreign interference, and socialist experimentation to reclaim its place on the global stage today.

No republic in history has shown more resiliency and adaptability than the United States of America. We have the tools and the ability to maintain our prosperity and stay a great nation. What we have to do is wake up, recognize our situation for what it is, acknowledge our challenges, and take steps to solve them.

CITIZEN WATCHDOGS

There's one basic political factor that I haven't given much attention to yet: you and me. It's amazing how closely Congress and the president pay attention to the facts during times when American citizens are paying attention to them. Presidents, with their bully pulpits, have the best opportunity to harness public opinion— Nixon invoking the "silent majority," Reagan directing an antitax uproar at Congress, and now Obama engaging in a public campaign for health care reform.

But there's no reason, in this electronic age, that we can't start a movement from the grass roots. For one thing, we can generate our own financial numbers. We at the Peterson Foundation are working to create a Federal Financial Irresponsibility Index. It will combine a number of key fiscal and financial factors into a single index that demonstrates the federal government's relative financial risk. We will only be able to take our analysis as far back as the 1990s because, believe it or not, the federal government did not issue consolidated financial statements until then.

We will acknowledge that some level of federal deficits, debt, reliance on foreign lenders, and other financial burdens can be acceptable. All that considered, we will come up with a figure that does provide an accurate picture of the relative risk of a "hard landing."

While we have not finalized our methodology, one thing is clear. Our nation's overall relative risk has increased dramatically in recent years. Based on projections by the Congressional Budget Office and on the automatic growth of the federal financial burden under current law, the risk is likely to get even worse if we continue on our present path.

We must recognize and begin to reduce rather than increase our nation's risk. In order to help people understand this need and to increase public pressure for policy makers to take action, we at the foundation have decided to publish the index periodically, so stay tuned. Everybody will be able to understand this number, and hopefully we can make it something that our representatives must pay attention to. Indices like these help to convey the simple and stark truth. If our representatives continue to sleep and fail to take steps to put our nation on a more prudent and sustainable path, our risk will continue to increase with the passage of time. And when will we pass a tipping point?

We are not condemned to repeat our mistakes. We can reassert our founding principles, return to our core values, and learn from history. We can resolve our many challenges and make sure that our future is better than our past. But it will require a long-term commitment to real transformation. It will also require the combined efforts of elected officials and millions of everyday citizens like you and me.

Four

OBAMA'S CHALLENGE

In 1981, Ronald Reagan shaped the politics of a generation when he declared, "Government is not the solution to our problem; government is the problem." What a change a generation can make. Barack Obama has, in his first year, sought to use the government to tackle the recession, regulate the financial system, save the auto industry, ensure universal health care, and beef up our education system, environmental protection, critical infrastructure, and scientific research, among other things. Not since LBJ's Great Society have we had a president who was as enthusiastic about government's ability to make a positive difference in people's lives.

In my view, the proper role for the federal government lies somewhere in between Reagan's and Obama's philosophies. We need a limited but effective government that focuses on the roles and functions that only government can and should perform. Government is necessary but it isn't the solution to many of our problems. That's what our nation's founders thought, and they were right.

Of course, all of President Obama's programs cost money, but as both candidate and president, Obama pledged to solve our long-term fiscal problems. Setting the tone in his inaugural address, Obama called for "a new era of responsibility" and imposed his own standard: "Those of us who manage the public's dollars will be held to account, to spend wisely, reform bad habits, and do our business in the light of day, because only then can we restore the vital trust between a people and their government."

Further signaling his seriousness about this issue, the president held a "Fiscal Responsibility Summit" at the White House early in his first term. He invited roughly a hundred people from government, business, labor, academia, and the not-for-profit sector, including Pete Peterson and me, to discuss our fiscal challenge, with breakout sessions on the budget process, Social Security, health care, tax reform, and procurement. All of these are certainly in the sweet spot of our problem, and they are all discussed in this book. The president wanted to emphasize that although it was necessary to spend hundreds of billions to bail us out of a major recession and address our other immediate challenges, he was determined to leave a legacy of fiscal responsibility.

When the president called on me, I took the opportunity to review the scary numbers—the government's balance sheet was about $11 trillion in the hole, and our obligations off the balance sheet were a much scarier $43 trillion. I also reminded him that he had called for a "grand bargain" to reform our budget process, Social Security, health care, and our tax systems. I told him candidly that I think it's going to take some type of extraordinary process that engages the American people and that provides for fast-track consideration of a package of needed reforms in Congress. I said that with his leadership, that could happen.

The president responded with vague assurances that he would indeed make these things a priority, and I went away encouraged but not satisfied. I was pleased to have a president who had pledged to take on the fiscal crisis and not punt tough choices to the next administration. Now, eight months later, I still have hope, but much has happened in the meantime to give me pause. The president has continued to say the right things. For example, in an interview with Fred Hiatt of *The Washington Post,* he publicly acknowledged that it may take a special commission to get this job done. But when will we get one?

Our financial markets showed signs of optimism in the summer of 2009 (though, of course, I can't be sure whether that's continued as you read this). The government's economic overseers spoke tentatively about signs of a recovery and a return to economic growth. Even housing prices in a number of cities were edging up. *The New York Times* suggested that Obama's massive stimulus spending had helped turn the tide and that historians may credit him (and the Federal Reserve) with reviving the economy.

I hope we're coming out of the woods. I love rising markets and economic growth as much as the next person. But short-term deficits and market swings are not what is threatening our future. The danger fundamentally comes from that ever-deepening federal financial hole. Ultimately, our economic health depends on our ability to tax and spend responsibly and with a focus on the future. A lot of factors are more important in this equation than short-term growth and optimism. I'm telling that to you now just as I told it to Congress in early 2001, when we had a balanced budget and our challenges existed beyond the typical ten-year budget horizon.

President Obama has talked the talk about our nation's long-term interests, recognizing our bad fiscal habits. "What we have done is kicked this can down the road," he said after his election victory. "We are now at the end of the road and are not in a position to kick it any further. We have to signal seriousness in this by making sure some of the hard decisions are made under my watch, not someone else's."

I am sure he was serious about that when he said it. But in his stimulus spending, his championing government control of General

Motors Corporation (aka Government Motors Corporation), and his first budget, he has shown few signs that he intends to engineer the type of fundamental transformation it will take to put us on a more prudent and sustainable path. For a president who shows a great awareness of language and takes great care in choosing his words, a lot of what the Obama administration says has not been consistent with its actions. More government is not the answer when government has already promised more than it can deliver.

We have to be vigilant with our presidents for the basic reason that they want to remain popular and get reelected. Toward the end of his first year in office, Obama was still campaigning so hard that he risked overexposure. Presidents tend to drop in popularity if they follow a path that requires them to deny things to various constituencies. Even if they try to take that path, they face the obstacles of competing agendas among their staff, the Congress, and a broad range of special-interest groups. What did Chief of Staff Rahm Emanuel mean, for example, when he said, "You never want a crisis to go to waste"? Did he mean that we need to make tough choices to put our nation's finances in order? Or was he talking about spending more on initiatives that Democrats have been promoting for a long time but haven't been able to get passed? Early indicators are that he may have had more spending in mind.

PRIORITY NUMBER ONE: THE RECESSION

In the January of President Obama's inauguration, the Congressional Budget Office estimated that we were facing a deficit of $1.2 trillion in the budget year ending September 30. That was his baseline—the amount he had to try to whittle down while also working to boost the global economy out of recession and addressing crises in financial institutions and the housing market. Not a very nice inauguration present, particularly considering that this was anything but a garden-variety recession.

The scope of the financial collapse that greeted the new administration essentially gave Obama an opportunity to do whatever he thought it took to get us out of it. And indeed, the spending he let loose to stimulate the economy, combined with other actions by the government and the Federal Reserve, seem to have had an effect. Nonetheless, our nation's financial condition has continued to deteriorate. In the spring of 2009, the deficit for the fiscal year was estimated to be $1.7 trillion, roughly $500 billion more than President Obama inherited from President Bush. (It ended up being $1.42 trillion for fiscal 2009.) The new president's stimulus spending had a lot to do with the spreading red ink—and the problem seemed to be getting worse.

We can't fault the president for having to raise spending to some degree, and some level of stimulus was both appropriate and necessary. Any new leader would have been compelled to use all the tools available to help jolt the economy out of severe recession—and the biggest of those tools is the power to spend lots of money. In evaluating President Obama's commitment to fiscal sanity, we need to look at the degree to which this spending was designed (1) for its immediate impact on the economy, and (2) to expire after a reasonable period of time.

By these tests, Obama's plan didn't pass muster. The president wanted some of the money for his own projects, and members of Congress had spending plans of their own. The result was a $787 billion package that included middle-class tax cuts and catchall spending on state aid, infrastructure, health care, education grants, alternative energy, and other Democratic priorities.

According to the Congressional Budget Office (CBO), only 23 percent of the spending and tax cuts were designed to hit the economy in fiscal 2009 (by September 30) and only about 30 percent in calendar 2009. And not all of it was temporary. Some of the spending extended government programs, some of it expanded them, and some required states to make multiyear spending commitments as a condition for accepting the additional assistance. In summary, the American Recovery and Reinvestment Act (popularly known as the stimulus bill) provided for $288 billion in tax relief and $499 billion in direct spending. The largest spending categories were related to state and local fiscal relief ($144 billion), infrastructure and science ($111 billion), protecting the economically vulnerable such as the unemployed ($81 billion), health care ($59 billion), and education and training ($53 billion).

You can't blame Obama alone for this excessive spending. As he was moving into office, the Democrats controlled both houses of Congress and the White House for the first time in fourteen years. That created a perfect storm for spending. Democrats coming to power were eager to satisfy pent-up demands for their programs just as the country needed a massive stimulus. Billions of dollars of careless spending, some of it destined to extend for years, was practically guaranteed as the Democrats pushed through the stimulus package in a rushed, haphazard way, while every special-interest group in town joined the feeding frenzy. Fresh from making promises of fiscal responsibility, Obama let it all go through, arguing that the economy needed the boost even if some of the spending was unwise.

I'm not writing to oppose children's preschool programs or health insurance for the unemployed. But committing to such new benefits without providing a way to pay for them is how we got into this mess in the first place. That's the problem at the root of our deficits: Nothing makes you more popular than providing a new benefit. It's easy to give people money. It's hard to take it away, even when you can't really afford the benefit.

MORE BAD SPENDING

In addition to signing the bloated stimulus package, President Obama signed a $410 billion omnibus spending bill for fiscal 2009—a bill that funds a wide range of programs Congress has approved. ("Omnibus" indeed.) The bill included an 8.3 percent increase in the prior base of spending for discretionary programs (that is, spending for things like defense and infrastructure, which Congress has control over). How can one justify such a significant increase in spending when core inflation is almost zero and when most businesses, governments, and not-for-profit entities are tightening their belts? This should not make us feel reassured about the president's commitment not to "kick the can down the road."

The omnibus bill also included a 10 percent increase in spending for the legislative branch and more than 8,500 "earmarks"—pet projects inserted by lawmakers—worth $7.7 billion. What about Obama's promise to be fiscally responsible? He let the earmarks and excessive spending go through, arguing that they were developed on President Bush's watch. However, Bush no longer had a veto pen (even though he had trouble finding it during his own time in office). President Obama did.

He could use a poor excuse like that only once. The $3.5 trillion fiscal 2010 budget is the Obama administration's first major annual spending document, and he owns it. On the plus side, Obama's numbers are more truthful and transparent than Bush's. It shows the costs of the Iraq and Afghanistan wars rather than putting them in supplementary appropriations, as Bush did, hiding these huge expenditures outside of the government's regular budget. Obama extends his budget projections for ten years rather than Bush's five, giving us a better idea of the long-term effects of our government's decisions.

That longer horizon shows more clearly the dangerous growth of our structural deficit—the built-in gap between what we will have to pay for social benefits and the revenue we will collect to pay for them. It also shows the cumulative damage caused by Bush's tax cuts. This is an important step, and Obama should be praised for it. Finally, Obama's first budget sets a goal to cut the deficit by more than half—to $533 billion—by 2013. It's good to have a goal.

That goal is nothing to cheer about, however, and neither is Obama's budget. It contains hundreds of billions of dollars in new spending for health care, education, and energy programs. But it lacks any major transformational reforms that might address our huge structural deficits. Even if Obama can't fix Social Security, Medicare, and other hemorrhaging programs once and for all, he must at the very least do something to stop the bleeding. For example, he could have pushed hard for the return to tough statutory budget controls after the economy turns around, but he didn't. Maybe he will in later budget proposals.

In fairness, Obama's plan proposes to squeeze savings, if modest ones, from Medicare, Medicaid, and other health programs by introducing more competitive bidding into Medicare, reducing planned provider reimbursements, and other steps. It also includes revenue from rolling back the Bush tax reductions for wealthy Americans and from limiting some of their tax deductions. This new money would go into a $635 billion reserve fund set aside to pay for health care reforms.

There are two problems with this reserve fund strategy. One is that $635 billion is not enough. The true cost of expanding health coverage as President Obama initially proposed was more than $1 trillion for the first ten-year period alone, according to independent estimates. The second problem is that the so-called "reserve fund" is a delusion, because no money is really being set aside for anything. The federal government has never had a "reserve fund" with one dime of real money in it. I'll explain the government mentality later in the book where I write about the Social Security "trust funds."

After ten years, under Obama's 2010 budget plan, the federal deficit would still amount to about 4 percent of the nation's economy, and that's too high. And it might go even higher. Obama's projections assume a rapid recovery from the recession, including 3.4 percent growth in 2010 and 5 percent over time. Others are not so optimistic. The Congressional Budget Office estimated 1.5 percent growth in 2010 (an estimate made before the stimulus), and the Blue Chip Consensus forecast predicted 1.8 percent at the time.

That may not look like a huge discrepancy, but as the president himself conceded, small differences add up to a lot of money over time. If his economic assumptions are too optimistic, the actual deficits are likely to be much higher. The Congressional Budget Office estimated that the actual ten-year budget deficits will be $2.03 trillion higher than original White House estimates, primarily due to differences in economic growth assumptions. Obama's budget director, Peter Orszag, conceded that deficits that high would be unacceptable and unsustainable.

In August 2009, the CBO and the Office of Management and Budget (OMB) released their updated projections of the budget deficit for fiscal 2009 and the next ten years. They contain both good news and bad news. On the positive side, the nonpartisan CBO estimated that the fiscal 2009 deficit will be about $1.6 trillion rather than the $1.7 trillion it estimated in the spring. (It ended up being $1.42 trillion for fiscal 2009.) On the negative side, the CBO raised its ten-year deficit estimates to more than $7.1 trillion, up from $4.4 trillion in the spring. That reinforces the idea that our primary problem is not the short term, it's our longer-term structural imbalances. The OMB's ten-year deficit number was even higher, at about $9 trillion, up from about $7 trillion in the spring. There's a difference between the CBO and OMB calculations. The CBO's are based on current law, whereas the OMB's are based on President Obama's proposal policies.

THE LANGUAGE OF SPENDING

With escalating deficit and debt levels like those the CBO and OMB show, one might ask, where precisely does the administration draw the line that defines the term "unacceptable"? And what does President Obama mean by "a new era of responsibility"? Based on these huge numbers, it's still the big spenders who are setting the parameters. To see that, all you have to do is compare what Obama's team said with what it actually did.

As the recession deepened throughout 2008, Harvard economist Larry Summers, who had served as Clinton's Treasury secretary, emphasized that Washington's stimulus package must be timely, targeted, and temporary. I had made similar comments in the past, as had others.

By the time Summers joined Obama's transition team, on his way to becoming the president's chief economic adviser, his tone had changed considerably. In one op-ed column, he called for a stimulus package that would help us recover from recession and serve also as "a down payment on our nation's long-term financial health." Summers used the term "invest," "investment," or "reinvestment" thirteen times in the article, all variations of that favorite Obama euphemism for spending.

Then there's Summers's term "down payment." What does that mean in Washington? Well, people who are fiscally responsible usually think it means taking steps to reduce the federal government's tens of trillions in liabilities and unfunded promises. But it looks like Summers and the Obama administration may have meant more debt-financed spending and an expanded role for the federal government. If so, hold on to your wallets.

Here's how to think of Washington's "investments." The federal government borrowed $787 billion as a "down payment" for the stimulus bill. That's right, there's not a dime of equity, and the entire amount was added to our national debt. Does that remind you of anything? How about all the Americans who made no down payments and took out subprime loans to finance homes they couldn't afford? Those irresponsible borrowing practices, abetted by all the middlemen making a quick buck, caused the subprime mortgage crisis. Now our government is acting like one of those irresponsible mortgagees.

So let me see if I have this right. In order to help us recover from our past borrow-and-spend excesses, the federal government is going to do more borrowing and spending, on a more massive scale, in part to fund additional expansions in the role of the federal government. Does that make sense to you? Now you know why I call Washington "the La La Land of the East." It's just not attached to the real world.

WHAT PEOPLE WANT

President Obama has to maneuver his way through a lot of constituencies, including Democratic senators and congress members, his own staff, and special-interest groups. Underneath it all, he may actually be a fiscal reformer. If he enacts major fiscal reforms, he will have one indispensable constituency on his side: public opinion. Ask the American people, and they will tell you overwhelmingly that our sustained fiscal health is fundamentally important. In fact, we at the Peterson Foundation did ask them. The foundation commissioned a rigorous national poll by Hart Research Associates and Public Opinion Strategies in late March 2009. We wanted to see whether the recent hard times had made people more likely to accept reforms. And the answer was yes.

Above all, Americans told us that they want to get the economy back on track. But their second priority for the Obama administration was somewhat surprising. They wanted the president and the Congress to address our escalating deficits and debt levels.

A cynic might suggest that it's easy to endorse fiscal responsibility—as long as the money to pay for it doesn't come out of your own pocket. Bill Clinton succeeded with the help of a strong economy; in the 1990s, we didn't feel that the government was picking our pockets. In the 2010s, our weak economy could work for Obama: We have seen what irresponsible spending can lead to, and it's scary. With the right leadership, Americans may be ready to accept tough choices to secure a better future.

You can't get a better consensus for reform than we found. In summary, 73 percent of Republicans rated our growing budget deficits and national debt as a very big threat, along with 72 percent of independents and 58 percent of Democrats. About 90 percent wanted Washington to take action to address these issues. Somewhat surprisingly, the respondents rated this issue as being more important than health care reform and middle-class tax cuts. Americans also saw escalating deficits and debt as a danger more serious than global warming and our declines in education and manufacturing. In our poll, public concern about our economic future even trumped fears of a rogue nation developing a nuclear weapon (see figure 4). That's what I call concern!

Yes, public opinion can shift quickly as the wind changes. If terrorists attacked us again on our home soil, the poll numbers would change. But my point is that in the early phase of his term, Obama had powerful public backing for the "grand bargain" on taxing and spending that, in January 2009, he said he wanted to achieve during his presidency.

Public concern continued to increase in succeeding months. In fact, it was manifest not just in more recent public opinion polls

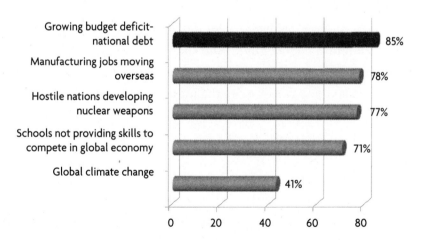

Figure 4 Voters' views on our nation's greatest threats. Hart Research Associates and Public Opinion Strategies poll, March 2009.

but in public anger during many town hall meetings during Congress's August 2009 recess. It's true that some of the assertions and actions by protesters in town hall meetings regarding the pending health care reform proposals were inaccurate, inappropriate, and irresponsible. However, people had a right to be concerned about out-of-control spending and about plans to further expand the federal government. I fully expect that public concern will increase more now that the August 2009 long-term deficit projections have been released and Washington pushes for even more health care entitlements.

We've heard other presidents make strong statements regarding fiscal responsibility. Even President Bush 43 pledged to be fiscally responsible. Boy, was he telling a whopper! Let's be fair to President Obama. It's still early in his first term. However, as of this writing, there is no plan to put a process in place to achieve a "grand bargain" or to seriously reform federal spending programs and tax policies. Hopefully, one will be coming soon—possibly as part of his fiscal 2011 budget proposal, which is due in February 2010.

Cracks are continuing to appear in our government's financial foundation. In the fall of 2009, the Federal Deposit Insurance Corporation, which insures our bank deposits, revealed that it faced serious cash-flow challenges. So did the Transportation Department's Highway Trust Fund. And the Social Security Administration disclosed that the retirement and survivors insurance program was expected to pay out more than it took in during 2010–11.

A WAY FORWARD

The job of putting our finances in order is not all Obama's, of course. When push comes to shove, all Americans have to do what's right to help ensure a better future. According to our poll, a lot of Americans still think Washington can address our escalat-

ing deficits by doing the relatively little things—eliminating earmarks, pulling out of Iraq, or ending the Bush tax cuts. This is
wrong.

And many Americans oppose changes that might affect them—
like raising the eligibility age for Social Security or Medicare. Left
to our worst instincts, in other words, after all the financial trauma
we have been through, we still want maximum services for minimum payments.

It's time to get real. There is a way forward out of this fiscal
mess, and it will make us all stronger, not weaker, over time. Let's
start with the reality of what I call the three rules of holes. First,
when you find yourself in a hole—especially if it's a multi-trillion-
dollar hole that is getting deeper every day—stop digging. Second,
you need to develop a good plan for climbing out. And third, once
you start making progress, you need to be sure that you can keep
from falling back in.

To get out of that hole, Washington needs to employ tough-love
principles right now. Rather than championing solutions, the
major parties are standing their ground. The Democrats resist dramatic reforms to Social Security, Medicare, and other benefits. The
Republicans resist raising taxes. Both sides happen to be wrong.
We must make our benefit programs affordable and sustainable,
and we must increase revenues above historical levels. We can find
ways to go through the back door on some of these changes—
trimming benefits for future retirees rather than present-day recipients, for example, and cracking down on tax breaks rather than
raising rates. But we have to clean up both sides of the budget—
income and outgo.

We don't need a nip and tuck. We need reconstructive surgery.
Most Americans love Social Security, Medicare, and the other programs that cushion us from life's hard landings, and many Americans rely upon them to a greater extent than they should. But we
must recognize the truth. These programs must be reformed if we

want to get on a prudent and sustainable fiscal path while also ensuring that the government will deliver on its promises in the future.

A president can't focus on providing all that people want, because they want too much, especially if they think someone else will pay for it. We need a president who will focus on the collective best interest of our nation both today and tomorrow. What do we really need, and what can we afford and sustain over time, and how should we pay for it? The president who brings real reform will answer these tough questions. And "We the People" need to follow that president.

Most of this requires no more than courage and common sense. In less than ten years I'll be eligible for Medicare, but should I receive significant premium subsidies for my optional Medicare coverage, as people whose lifetime earnings are near the poverty level do? The answer is clearly no, but unless the program is reformed, that is what will happen.

Frankly, our country cannot afford to give people like me benefits we do not really need or deserve. The government safety net should be designed first and foremost to protect those who are in need. It's fine to give others the option to buy into certain social insurance programs, but not to the extent of subsidizing middle- and upper-income people, especially when the bill will be paid by future generations.

Rethinking social programs is only part of the challenge. President Obama also must show some tough love to make our government more cost effective. A reform government must streamline the Pentagon, for one thing, to reduce the number of units and bureaucratic layers, rationalize weapons systems for the post–Cold War world, and reform the acquisition and contracting systems, abolishing the inappropriate roles that contractors currently play. President Obama has said he wants to reduce waste in the Pentagon and eliminate a range of federal programs that don't work or are outdated. To his credit, during his first eight months in office, he called for trimming back or dramatically changing several weapons programs, including the F-22 fighter/ground attack tactical aircraft and the Army's Future Combat System, to more reasonable levels. This is a positive step, but much more needs to be done. Has he unveiled any major transformational reforms that will serve to reengineer the foundation of government and put us on a more prudent and sustainable fiscal path by the time you're reading this book? If not, when will he?

We need a broad swath of reforms, including transformations of the way our government and politics work. You will read about those in the rest of this book. The place to start is with common-sense reforms to our tax and spending policies.

We have a model in our own backyard, as I learned during a September 2009 meeting with Canada's comptroller general, Rod Monette. Canada makes a clear public accounting of its fiscal condition—which is healthier than ours. Among other things, Canada puts limits on what it pays for health care, and so should the United States. There are plenty of other useful models of fiscal responsibility, if we look around the world.

Let's all hope that the normal processes of government finally work this time—that President Obama comes up with effective reforms and that Congress improves them and passes them into law. Do you worry that won't happen? I sure do.

There is another way, outside of the normal flow of government, that will guarantee first, that serious reforms find their way to the national agenda, and second, that Congress will consider them. We need a Fiscal Future Commission that will engage a meaningful and representative number of the American people and come up with a reform plan for consideration by the Congress and the president. Don't roll your eyes at the thought of another government commission. This would not be another Inside-the-Beltway-Andrews-Air-Force-Base-Trust-Us Commission. The time for such approaches is long gone. Washington is sick, and the cure has to be imported from the real world. This commission would do far more than give advice. Its reform proposals would be spliced into the legislative process as a way to turbocharge the kind of comprehensive changes we need.

This commission would be created by law to explore a range of budget, spending, tax, and other reforms. It would also educate and engage the public in an effort to identify possible reforms and engineer a more radical restructuring of the federal government. The group would include elected representatives and administration officials. It would also include several capable and credible experts who have no other connection to government and who are willing to dedicate a significant amount of their time to restore fiscal sanity and help save our future.

A properly designed commission would venture far outside Washington's Beltway to conduct town hall forums with a representative group of Americans around the nation, and it would leverage the Internet to get millions of people involved in needed reforms. Everything would be on the table—health and retirement programs, tax policy, and budget rules.

Ultimately, the commission would present a package of recommendations to Congress that our legislators could not ignore because so many of us would support them. In fact, the rules setting up the commission would require Congress to hold hearings and vote on the body's recommendations—if a predesignated supermajority of commission members endorsed them. And Congress would not be able to amend the commission's recommendations in a way that hurt the fiscal bottom line.

If the commission showed it could be successful, it would work wonders. In my view, it should focus first on saving Social Security. A consensus for that reform is within reach, as those of us in the Social Security breakout group at President Obama's Fiscal Responsibility Summit agreed. A major Social Security reform would give us a big win that would push us on to more difficult policy issues.

Once we start to climb out of the fiscal hole, we have to make sure we don't fall back in. President Obama needs to bring back the budgetary controls of the Bush 41 and Clinton era and impose some new ones as well. When mandatory spending programs or tax breaks increase to a certain level, the government needs a trigger forcing their scrutiny, even if those programs are sacred cows such as Social Security, Medicare, federal pension and retiree health benefits, the home mortgage interest deduction, and the individual exclusion of employer-provided health care insurance from taxation. Our social programs are growing unhindered. And the federal government is losing more than a trillion dollars a year in revenue due to a range of tax breaks that are also on autopilot. We need to put our hands back on the controls. We need to force disclosure of the longer-term costs—beyond ten years—of major spending and tax proposals before they are voted on. The president's budget should be required to project ahead for at least ten years and contain an express fiscal goal. In addition, the president should be required to issue a long-range fiscal sustainability report—looking forty years out—at least every five years.

We have to avoid finding new ways to waste money. We should consider creating a capital budget to better manage government building projects, for example. But we must make sure that we base the projects on merit and that we control their costs.

We also need a better way to understand and monitor exactly what we're getting when a piece of major legislation passes. We need rules that will force Congress to define the outcomes-based objectives of the legislation in ways we can measure. Then it becomes the executive branch's job to implement the law as efficiently and effectively as possible. This includes specifying appropriate criteria for who should receive federal money and what can and cannot be done with the money. Unfortunately, this didn't happen with the first $350 billion installment of the $700 billion Troubled Asset Relief Program (TARP). It also didn't happen with much of the stimulus spending. If the process works as it should, we citizens should understand exactly what a law is intended to do and be able to measure whether it succeeds. Coupled with the right kind of systems and controls, such a process will result in significant savings, improved performance, and enhanced accountability.

As of this writing, it's way too early to evaluate Obama's record. However, it's clear that he was too trusting of Congress's ability to handle the stimulus bill, the fiscal 2009 budget, and health care reform. He must exert more presidential leadership and provide more specifics on what he is for and against on these types of major issues.

Barack Obama will be leading our government until at least 2013, and it's up to us to monitor his policies during these crucial years. I hope this monitoring will come from all parts of the political spectrum, and in particular from the real world outside of Washington, D.C. I hope you now have some ideas of how to measure the administration's progress. Most of all, I hope and pray that President Obama will take the actions necessary to turn things around.

Five

SAVE SOCIAL SECURITY FIRST

We have to do something to save Social Security.

You've heard that before. When we talk about our government's financial problems in this country, we never (well, unless you're me) shout, "Save our fiscal integrity!" We speak in terms of the government programs that serve us, and in that lot Social Security is an evergreen. In fact, calls to save Social Security have become a dangerous political cliché—dangerous because you hear these alarms so often that it's hard to take them seriously; it's the political equivalent of crying wolf. Prophets of doom can rant all they want, but retired Americans don't really believe their Social Security checks will stop coming, and if you're not yet retired, I'll bet you don't spend a lot of time awake at night worrying about getting that check when your time comes. (That may not be true for some young people, who are beginning to worry—unnecessarily, I think—that Social Security will not be there when they retire.)

Social Security is arguably the most successful federal program, and the Social Security Administration is one of the most effective agencies in our government. In fact, it regularly receives customer satisfaction ratings that rival top private-sector service companies. In spite of its growing burdens, Social Security is actually in the best shape of the major social programs I'll write about in this book.

That's why I am analyzing it first. For the next few years, Social Security is fine; but if we take seriously our stewardship responsibility for the Americans who come after us—a key principle of this book—Social Security is already setting off alarm signals. We can be as complacent as we want to be, but the unfunded obligations are mounting and somebody someday will have to pay the price. I've noted that the disability program is already in a negative cash flow position and the retirement and survivors income program is expected to have a negative cash flow in 2010–11. If we keep on doing nothing until the trust funds that finance the program run dry in 2037, monthly benefits will have to be cut about 24 percent across the board, and the cuts will get deeper after that.

It's easy to see what's wrong with the program, and the fixes are commonsense and obvious—no problem for anybody in the sensible center. Social Security is a test case of how well we Americans can face facts and address large, known, and growing problems before a crisis reaches our doorstep. Reforming it would demonstrate that we have finally recognized we can't get something for nothing. I know the issues well, having served as a trustee of Social Security and Medicare from 1990 to 1995. We can make Social Security so secure that you will never have to hear that old cliché again.

You and I have to do our part by acknowledging realities: Number one, we're living longer, our economy has changed, and Social Security should be adjusted accordingly. Number two, we have to save more ourselves to help secure our own retirement, especially if we don't want to work longer.

Let's take a few minutes to look at the scope and history of our

Social Security problem. Then I'll outline a reform program that will ensure Social Security's promises are matched by enough funds to make good on them.

ROOSEVELT'S MODEST DESIGN

Our government retirement benefits have European roots. The first social insurance pension system emerged in Germany in the 1870s, the creation of Chancellor Otto von Bismarck, who was the kind of brilliant politician who could make a liberal political promise that was fiscally conservative. Bismarck saw his society changing to the detriment of Germany's senior citizens. The industrial revolution had eliminated some of the manual jobs that had previously provided their livelihood. In response, Bismarck promised a modest state pension to Germans who lived to age seventy (later dropped to sixty-five). At the time, the average life expectancy of Germans was fifty-five. As a result, very few people received the benefit, and those who did generally were unemployable and needed the money.

Fast-forward to 1935 and you come to the inception of the Social Security program in the United States. President Roosevelt faced a different social problem. America was still in the grips of a depression; unemployment levels were very high, as were poverty rates among senior citizens. As one of his key New Deal initiatives, Roosevelt decided to provide a safety net for people who weren't able to support themselves, using Bismarck's system as one model.

This safety net—Social Security—actually includes two programs. The larger, the better known, and the one that serves as the primary focus of this chapter is the retirement and survivors income program. It provides retirement income to eligible participants and, after they pass away, to their dependents. There is also a disability income program to help those who lose their ability to work before reaching retirement age.

Social Security was never intended to be the sole source of income for retirees and the disabled. Like the foundation of a house, it was designed to serve merely as the base of a secure retirement, supplemented by employer-sponsored pension and disability programs as well as personal savings.

Its financing was straightforward. Working Americans would contribute payroll taxes to special trust funds. (These are the "FICA" deductions from your paycheck, the acronym standing for Federal Insurance Contributions Act.) Money from the funds, in turn, would support monthly payments to retirees and disabled workers. This system worked fine in the early years of Social Security. America had a lot more workers than retired people, and the trust funds generated healthy surpluses.

In those early years, with so many workers contributing, most retirees garnered far more in Social Security benefits than they had ever paid in payroll taxes. The first person to receive Social Security benefits, in 1940, was Ida May Fuller. She paid only about $23 in taxes to the Social Security program, but received approximately $22,000 in benefits during her lifetime. That sounds like a pretty good deal to me. However, now the system has matured, and the ratio of workers to retirees has declined from 16:1 in 1950 to 3.3:1 today. Those deals are gone forever.

Even from the start, our program was not quite as brilliantly conceived as Bismarck's. By the time the U.S. Social Security system was established in the summer of 1935, average life expectancy in America was about sixty-five; nonetheless, Washington adopted Germany's sixty-five, rather than a later age, as the eligibility level for full retirement benefits. That guaranteed the program would enroll a greater percentage of senior citizens than might have been necessary. In addition, the program's administrators later decided that people could obtain reduced early retirement benefits at age sixty-two, putting even more retirees into the system.

Problems arose as America's demographic portrait changed. The surge of baby boomers, born after World War II, had fewer of their own children, and the national workforce began to age. The equation shifted toward fewer workers paying taxes and more retirees receiving benefits. And those benefits kept increasing. In 1950, Congress approved the first cost-of-living adjustment in Social Security to keep the benefits ahead of inflation. In 1972, these so-called COLAs were made automatic, pegged to an index that measured inflation. Unfortunately, these increased benefits were not adequately funded.

The payroll taxes that finance Social Security are currently 6.2 percent, imposed on both the employee and the employer. The payroll taxes are levied on each worker's salary only up to a certain annual dollar amount, usually known as the "wage base cap"; any earnings above this amount are exempt from payroll taxes for Social Security. Just as the COLAs go up automatically, so does the wage cap; in 2009, it rose from $102,000 to $106,800. But, consistent with the story I'm telling throughout this book, the increase in funding does not cover the increase in the cost of benefits—and as you look into the future, the picture gets scarier and scarier.

ALARM BELLS

The first real trouble emerged in 1975, when the government realized that within four years it would not be collecting enough payroll taxes to finance Social Security benefits. Congress raised taxes and trimmed benefits enough to hold off disaster. Still, by 1983 the alarm bells were ringing again—the trust funds were running out of money. To put more permanent reforms in place, President Reagan appointed a commission led by Alan Greenspan (before he became chairman of the Federal Reserve). The pressure was on to come up with a rescue plan and for Congress to adopt it—fast. In fact, the combined Social Security trust funds were set to run dry within weeks. If they had gone to zero, the monthly Social Security checks would not have gone out on time. Can you imagine the outcry and the political consequences if tens of millions of Americans had not received their Social Security checks on time? Now that would have been a crisis!

The commission's recommendation was essentially an endorsement of a private deal between President Reagan and Speaker of the House Tip O'Neill. Congress voted to tax some Social Security benefits, and to add federal workers to the payroll-tax roster for the first time. The goal was to help ensure that the program could deliver on its promises for the next seventy-five years. (Not that the country will disappear after seventy-five years; that's simply the time frame Social Security trustees use to measure the long-term health of the system. It covers three generations of Americans as well as the likely life span of all persons currently paying into the system.)

For the most part, the Greenspan Commission did its job. It prompted Congress and the president to act, and it gave them a political cover to do so. And its recommendations did buy the program time. The commission did not, however, propose one very important yet controversial change: increasing the retirement eligibility age in light of longer life expectancies. It took Representative Jake Pickle (D-TX), chairman of the Social Security subcommittee of the powerful House Ways and Means Committee, to do that. Pickle had the courage to offer an amendment that gradually increased the normal retirement age from sixty-five to sixty-seven. And guess what? His amendment passed. Most members realized that it was the right thing to do even if it wasn't popular. That was a true victory of courage and leadership—Jake did the right thing even though it might send shock waves through his political career.

The conventional wisdom is that Social Security is the "third rail" of American politics. The idea is that any elected federal official who seeks to modify the popular program will pay a painful political price—like touching the electrified third rail of a subway system. Well, the third rail did not zap Jake Pickle. He kept his

House seat and went on to serve eleven more years, retiring only after he decided he had served long enough. (Jake was one politician who knew when he had served long enough.)

Since 1983, other administrations have tried to strengthen Social Security, with less success. In the late 1990s, President Bill Clinton tried the collaborative approach, reaching beyond Washington to educate and engage the American people. He asked the Concord Coalition, a nonprofit group that promotes fiscal responsibility, to hold a series of town hall sessions on reform along with AARP, the leading advocacy organization for people over fifty years old. Concord and AARP teamed up with AmericaSpeaks, a group that organizes town-hall-style meetings on public issues, to conduct several meetings across the country. The sessions were intended to inform people and generate ideas and to help prepare the way for comprehensive Social Security reform. I was asked by Concord and AARP to be the lead "truth teller" and to help make the case for comprehensive Social Security reform.

We held several major regional forums, each attended by President Clinton or Vice President Al Gore. Then the Clinton-Gore administration sponsored a White House conference on Social Security that drew members of Congress from both major parties as well as representatives from key stakeholder groups, including me. The conference reviewed the results of the outside-the-Beltway effort and reinforced the need for timely reform—or as the Clinton-Gore administration put it, to "Save Social Security First."

The Clinton process proved to be very effective. The outside-the-Beltway sessions, combined with the Clinton administration's quieter inside-the-Beltway efforts, set the stage for comprehensive reform that likely would have involved maintaining a basic benefit program and adding supplemental individual accounts, among other changes. That would have been a huge leap forward for America and a positive legacy for President Clinton.

There was only one problem, and it was a big one: Monica

Lewinsky and the blue dress incident. As Clinton faced scandal and impeachment, he had to spend his political capital on staying in office rather than on reforming Social Security. Despite all our work, there was no change in the status quo. Nonetheless, the process that Clinton and his staff set in motion, both in Washington and around the country, demonstrated the right way to go about achieving comprehensive Social Security and other key reforms. And it showed that Americans are ready to take change seriously if you go about it the right way.

In 2005, fresh from his reelection victory, President Bush also tried to reform Social Security. Unfortunately, his approach was flawed in at least three ways. First, he did not employ an open and inclusive process like Clinton's to help write his reform agenda and to build a consensus for timely action. The members appointed to his Social Security Reform Commission were required to agree in advance to support individual retirement accounts for workers in addition to the monthly checks to retirees. These individual accounts were to be an integral part of overall Social Security reform—even if such accounts had to be funded through more federal borrowing. Bush was unable to get any high-level elected Democrats to join him in his reform process. Furthermore, Bush's outside-the-Beltway public events were largely staged with crowds of screened supporters.

Second, Bush founded his reform process on the concept of an "ownership society." That is, he believed that people should have more control over how to invest their government retirement funds. That approach was based largely on his own political philosophy rather than on the needs and interests of Social Security participants themselves. The fact is, most Americans need Social Security, and they have come to rely on their inflation-indexed monthly benefit payment as an essential part of their retirement security plan.

Bush and his advisers should have studied the hierarchy of

needs devised by psychologist Abraham Maslow in the 1940s. Maslow pointed out that the most basic human need is self-preservation—and that is what Social Security is all about. The pinnacle of human need is self-actualization, according to Maslow. Living in America gives us an unparalleled opportunity to reach for that goal on our own.

Third, Bush's reform plan would have added more than $1 trillion in additional deficits and debt burdens at the federal level over the short to medium term—this at a time when America had already returned to deficits and increasing debt levels after several years of surpluses and even some reduction in debt.

Bush's flawed reform process and plan produced predictable results. After more than two hundred taxpayer-funded public events, about sixty of which either he or Vice President Dick Cheney attended, public support for the president's reforms had dropped below what it had been before the first event was held. I would call that failing a market test.

THE TRUST FUND CON

You could look at each of these reform efforts from a different perspective. For one thing, as Rahm Emanuel so helpfully reminded us, a crisis helps. The reforms of the 1970s and 1980s worked because Social Security faced imminent crises; in the 1990s and the decade after, no such crises existed. But I look at the record another way. We have shown that we can muster the political will to reform a major social program, if only in a patchwork way. Now it's time to fix Social Security for good—far beyond the seventy-five-year measure the trustees and accountants use.

That's because—I'll say it again—Social Security is in trouble. According to the Social Security Trustees Report, the Social Security program was in a $7.7 trillion hole as of January 1, 2009. That means Washington would have needed $7.7 trillion on that date, invested at prevailing rates, to deliver for the next seventy-five years on the promises that the federal government has made. But we actually need much more than that to keep Social Security healthy, because it will experience larger and larger deficits both in the near future and beyond the seventy-five-year accounting horizon. As of January 1, 2009, that number—the amount we would need to invest to ensure the sustainability of the program for seventy-five years and beyond—was $15.1 trillion. How much of this huge sum do we have invested in real liquid and transferable assets today—that is, how much in actual money? Zero, zip, cero, nada, nothing!

The truth is that the government's Social Security guarantee is one huge unfunded promise. How can this be? I have mentioned the Social Security "trust funds," where our payroll taxes go. All this money is transmitted to the federal government and credited to the Social Security trust funds. You would logically assume that these funds would have hard assets that have been saved and invested to cover the program's future costs. However, rather than saving the money and investing it in a diversified pool of real and readily marketable assets, the government spends it and provides "special-issue" government securities in return.

Just consider what actually goes into those funds. First there are the numbers reported in government financial statements. According to those numbers, Washington had issued approximately $2.4 trillion in special-issue U.S. government securities that had been credited to the Social Security trust fund as of January 1, 2009. The computer records documenting these securities are held in a locked file cabinet in West Virginia. But there is a reason they are called special-issue securities, and it's not good. Unlike regular government bonds, which people like us and the Chinese government can buy, these special-issue bonds cannot be sold; in other words, they are government IOUs that the government has issued to itself, to be paid back later—with interest. Imagine if you or I

could sit around writing IOUs to ourselves that were worth something. Great way to make a living.

Washington says that we can count on these bonds because they are backed by the full faith and credit of the United States government, which guarantees both principal and interest. But—believe it or not—under current federal accounting principles, the government does not consider these bonds to be liabilities—which is another way of saying the government doesn't really think that it's our money.

Think about that for a minute. If you or I lend the government money by buying a bond, the government has to pay us back with interest. In other words, that bond is a government liability. But when it comes to the Social Security trust funds, the government is saying the special-issue securities it deposits are not a liability—in other words, they're basically worth nothing at all. Now get this: The trust funds report these securities as assets on the annual reports that they provide to the public. Does that sound like wanting to have your cake and eat it too? Con artists of the world, I hope you're taking notes.

In my view, these bonds should be treated as liabilities, and their value should be counted as part of our debt-to-GDP ratio. After all, they are backed by the full faith and credit of the federal government, and I do not believe the federal government will default on them.

Under the current scheme, the Social Security program has been running large surpluses since the reforms of 1983. But in actuality, Washington has spent those surpluses every year on other government activities. That is one way the government can reduce its public borrowing and keep interest rates down.

To say the least, the federal government's accounting for these funds understates both its total liabilities and its annual operating deficits. That brings us to another clever bit of Washington wordsmithing: the "unified deficit." In public reporting, the government takes the real operating deficit, $638 billion in fiscal 2008, and subtracts the nonexistent amount credited to the Social Security trust funds, $183 billion in fiscal 2008. This "unified" figure—$455 billion—makes the federal budget deficit seem smaller than it actually is. And they have been doing this for many years.

These accounting tricks would never be allowed in the real world, where trust funds are subject to stringent accounting rules and fiduciary standards. In essence, Washington is playing a massive con game—collecting your Social Security taxes, spending that money for its own purposes, and accounting for it in trust funds that are largely a fiction. A more proper description would be "trust-the-government funds." Or as my boss, Pete Peterson, would say, "You can't trust them, and they aren't funded." Just another example of how words used in Washington don't have the same meaning they have in Webster's dictionary.

Don't worry, the reforms of the 1980s are still keeping the system above water. Monthly benefits should be paid in full for at least another three decades. However, the Social Security program will begin to pay out more than it takes in much sooner than that. The retirement and survivors income program expects its payments to exceed its revenues in 2010 and 2011. That will happen because revenue has declined during the recession—while at the same time, more people are retiring. When the federal government has to start cashing in the special-issue securities in the trust funds in order to pay benefits, it will have to raise taxes, cut benefits, and/or sell real bonds to the public in order to raise real money for retirees receiving benefits. If the government issues more public debt—in part to attract more foreign investors—that will likely increase our foreign dependency.

AVOIDING A CRISIS

We have no alternative but to keep Social Security strong. Approximately 35 percent of current retirees rely on Social Security for over 90 percent of their retirement income. For these people above all, we have to make sure that Social Security's "safety net" promise is kept.

Yet the demographic time bomb keeps ticking. If we do nothing, the system will run dry again and the government will be forced to slap together new emergency reforms. Assuming that we will not cut benefits drastically, we will be looking at the only alternative: further tax increases for our children and grandchildren.

Here's the bottom line: Social Security does not face a crisis immediately, because, as I noted earlier, the government will honor its special-issue securities. It does, however, face those $7.7-trillion-and-growing unfunded obligations that should be addressed sooner rather than later. Due to interest costs and projected demographic trends, these obligations grow by hundreds of billions each year that action is not taken. The disability program is in much worse financial shape than the retirement and survivors program. It began experiencing a negative cash flow in 2005, and its trust fund is expected to become exhausted in 2020. Historically, the disability fund has borrowed from the retirement and survivors fund when necessary. But that doesn't solve its financing problem. It only defers it.

One major lesson from past reform efforts is clear. If we want to make major program changes, jury-rigged reforms will not do. We will have to crank up the government reform machine again, probably in the form of the Fiscal Future Commission I proposed in the last chapter. I'll give you my views on how that process should play out later in the book.

We have to change more than the program. We have to change our attitudes. To get Social Security working again as its originators intended, we have to renew the American practice of saving for our own retirement.

In the late 1980s, we Americans saved an average of 7.3 percent of our disposable income. But then came the stock boom of the 1990s and the housing boom of the decade that followed. We felt rich, credit was easy to get—and we spent and spent. Our personal savings rate plummeted to less than 2 percent in 2005. (See figure 5.) By early 2007, at the height of the market bubble, the savings rate stood at an anemic 0.7 percent. After the bubble popped in 2007–08, not surprisingly, our savings rate increased as home equity and the stock market declined dramatically. By the summer of 2009, the individual savings rate had grown to over 5 percent. But you get the long-range picture: When times are good, many individuals spend more than they take home—becoming debtor citizens of our debtor nation.

This savings drought is another major reason Social Security has become indispensable. A government-funded retirement income plan is vital for Americans who are not saving for their own retirement. Yet much more than Social Security is at stake. Savings—generated by the government, by private enterprises, and by individuals—represent the seed corn of our future. With saving comes investing, which contributes to research and development, which results in innovation, productivity increases, process im-

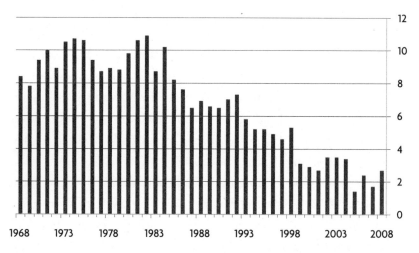

Figure 5 U.S. personal savings rate as a percentage of disposable income. Personal savings rates increased to over 5 percent in the summer of 2009. It remains to be seen whether this will be temporary or lasting.

provements, and quality enhancements. From these come increased employment and wages, and from these an improvement in our standard of living. As Alan Greenspan has said, "Without savings there is no future." I think that sums it up pretty well.

Social Security's designers intended it to be supplemented by employer pension plans and personal savings. As Roosevelt himself said, "We shall make the most lasting progress if we recognize that Social Security can furnish only a base upon which each one of our citizens may build his individual security through his own individual efforts."

Yet these nongovernmental efforts have consistently come up short. Company pension plans have never covered enough people. Today, about 50 percent of the workforce is covered by a private plan, a percentage that has not changed much in the past forty years. At the same time, despite the recent uptick in savings, the United States still has one of the lowest savings rates of any industrialized nation.

In our system, people who do save probably don't do much to take the pressure off Social Security. They tend to be better off financially—saving money mainly because they have more than they need to spend. Their retirements are generally more secure, even if recent market declines have made many 401(k) plans look more like 201(k) plans.

The government has tried to encourage personal thrift, offering numerous tax incentives for people to save. A significant percentage of savers put money aside to take advantage of these programs, which include pension plans, 401(k)s, individual retirement accounts, health savings accounts, and the like. But the impact of these programs is questionable, since those incentives actually cost the U.S. Treasury more than $120 billion a year.

Such tax-advantaged saving has become more common now that employers are allowed to automatically enroll their employees in private pension plans such as 401(k)s and similar offerings. Employees have to opt out of the savings plan rather than opting in. Don't get me wrong; I believe automatic enrollment is a good idea and will generate some incremental savings. It will also help to ensure that more employees take advantage of employer matching contributions. But at the same time, I do not see automatic enrollment as a major leap forward in our effort to boost our overall savings rate. After all, as I said above, these programs cover only about half of all workers.

We need to consider other ways to increase our savings and to make sure that people who actually will need the money after they quit working are among those who save. One answer might be to implement an automatic savings plan as part of comprehensive Social Security reform. After all, as my mother often said, "Once you touch the money, you will spend the money." Nowadays, many people spend it more than once!

SOME COMMONSENSE PROPOSALS

Increasing our savings rate will take some of the pressure off Social Security, but won't save it. We do need a government reform plan—and hopefully a better one than we've had in the past.

The reform process must have integrity: It must be nonpartisan, fact-based, inclusive, and transparent. Whatever we do will be controversial, because the system needs to change and humans don't like to change. There will be inevitable controversy over specific reform proposals; we don't need an additional controversy over whether the reform process itself is fair. If we get it wrong, we will be fighting a two-front war—one over substance and one over process. As Germany found out the hard way twice during the twentieth century, it's very hard to win a two-front war.

As we consider an appropriate way forward to reform Social Security, we should remember that other countries are ahead of us in making changes to their pension programs. Australia, New

Zealand, Canada, the United Kingdom, and Chile have already taken steps to make their systems more sustainable. Some of their efforts can be used to inform our own reform proposals, while others are more radical and therefore not likely to be politically feasible in the United States.

We don't have to change Social Security radically to make it secure and sustainable. The challenge is to make enough adjustments to properly finance it for seventy-five years and beyond. Yes, we need to make changes that recognize demographic realities and that ensure solvency indefinitely. We also need to respect our values of thrift, saving for the future, and passing on a better world to the next generation. Here are a few suggestions for how we can balance Social Security's promises with enough revenue to pay for them.

Benefits

- Focus on people who are most in need. Provide a new higher-level floor benefit for Americans who have worked at least thirty years to ensure they will not live in poverty. This will serve to strengthen the social safety net.
- Do not eliminate Social Security benefits for higher-income individuals but reduce the relative benefit for middle- and upper-income persons through progressive wage indexing or otherwise. This would ensure that benefits are better targeted to those in need without allowing Social Security to become a welfare program.
- Trim cost-of-living adjustments. A modest reduction, 0.5 percent or less, in these annual postretirement increases, possibly targeted to certain middle- and upper-income beneficiaries, would boost the reform effort while also helping to ensure that better-off retirees contribute to a sensible Social Security solution.

- Raise the normal and the early retirement eligibility ages on a gradual basis, and require that they keep pace with increases in life expectancy. A relatively modest increase—for example, from sixty-seven to seventy for the normal retirement age, and from sixty-two to sixty-five for the early retirement age—would have a significant impact, and the change could be implemented over a twenty-year period. An allowance could be made for manual laborers who can't continue to do heavy work as they grow older. These workers could access the disability program until they reach the normal retirement age. In combination, these changes would help to reduce and offset revenue losses caused by the slower growth of the workforce.
- Allow individuals to defer their Social Security benefits to any age they choose and increase their monthly benefit based on life-expectancy tables. This would encourage people to work longer.

Revenues

- Increase tax revenue. Keep the payroll tax rate at the current level of 6.2 percent but raise the cap on taxable wages from the 2009 level of $106,800 per person to around $150,000. This would be less than the historical dollar level at which 90 percent of total wage income would be subject to the Social Security payroll tax ($171,900 in 2009).

Savings

- Require supplemental savings accounts. An additional 2 or 3 percent payroll deduction would go into an individual account for each worker. Individuals would have several professionally managed investment options to choose from along the lines of the Federal Thrift Savings Plan, which is used now for federal elected officials and employees. This would help our overall savings rate while providing a meaningful preretirement death benefit and supplemental post-retirement benefits.

That's it. None of these ideas is particularly radical or new. The changes could be phased in so that people who have already retired or are nearing retirement—those who are between fifty-five and sixty years old, perhaps—would not be affected in any significant way. Yet these adjustments would result in a solvent, sustainable, secure, and more savings-oriented Social Security program. They would also secure a larger benefit for every generation of Americans than its members might be expecting to receive given the program's current troubles.

If reforms like these are necessary, sensible, and feasible, then what are we waiting for? It's called leadership, and hopefully we'll get some soon. Achieving Social Security reform would be a solid start toward our nation's return to a prudent fiscal path and would also help to ensure that the federal government can deliver on the promises that it makes. Should we expect any less from our government? Then why aren't we demanding that it act?

To demonstrate how far out of control Washington is in connection with federal spending, in October 2009, President Obama asked the Congress to authorize an ad-hoc payment of $250 each for Social Security beneficiaries. He did this because the official cost-of-living adjustment formula did not justify any increase in monthly benefits. This was a very troubling $13 billion spending proposal. It represented blatant political pandering that would only serve to further mortgage our future. It also ignored the fact that the poverty level among seniors is lower than in other segments of the population.

Six

CURING HEALTH CARE

I f there's one thing that could bankrupt America, it's out-of-control health care costs. It's no coincidence that President Obama chose this as his signature issue, nor that debate about it has dominated the media since he began to push for comprehensive health care reform.

Health care reform is another of those perennials of American politics. Theodore Roosevelt called for comprehensive health care reform while running for a third term in 1912, and Harry Truman made a big issue of it during his presidency, to no avail. President Truman lived long enough to attend the 1965 ceremony at which President Johnson signed Medicare into law. President Clinton tried to achieve comprehensive health care reform early in his presidency, without success. Most recently, George W. Bush expanded Medicare to include prescription drug coverage but made no attempt to achieve universal coverage.

It's easy to see why this issue keeps coming back to center stage. America's health care system (if you can call it a system) is among the most expensive on Earth, yet it fails to cover tens of millions of us and generates below average results in many cases, unless you happen to be rich. In some ways, it's the worst of both worlds— costing too much and doing a poor job. These problems are growing, and that's why the disaster in the making has once again captured Washington's attention. As Obama has put it: "The cost of our health care has weighed down our economy and the conscience of our nation long enough."

We already know this from our own experiences. Everybody has a story about bad health care. My wife and I got to see the system in action within the past few years, after Mary had an auto accident. While she was driving in the middle of the day, she fainted at the wheel and had a head-on collision with a pickup truck. Fortunately, she had just started moving after a traffic light changed, and she wasn't going too fast. That bit of luck, combined with our car's outstanding engineering, resulted in significant damage to the vehicle, but not a scratch on Mary.

After the accident, her primary care physician and a number of specialists subjected her to every test they could think of in an effort to find out why she had fainted. Despite running a battery of tests, almost all of them paid for by our insurance, the doctors never discovered the cause.

In her final appointment, the doctor ordered three more tests, the last he could think of. He wanted to do everything he could to try to find out what the problem was. While I certainly appreciated his wanting to help my wife, I was troubled by his reply when I asked how much the tests would cost. He said he had no idea and that we shouldn't worry because our insurance would cover it. I reminded him how insurance really works. Namely, the insurance company may pay the bill today, but we will pay the costs eventually. This seemed to be news to him. In his world, ordering every test imaginable, regardless of its usefulness or, shall we say, any fiscal considerations, was part of the routine. And what went unsaid was that in ordering more tests he made himself more money and reduced his risk of being sued. The total cost of all of the procedures he tried? Nearly $20,000.

I think it's safe to say that few people would have even questioned the doctor; if a loved one is sick, we want to do everything we can, no matter how low the odds it will actually help to get him or her better. Combine our incentive to try everything with the doctor's incentive to make money and avoid being sued and you can see what the problem is. Project these wasteful practices throughout our entire health care system—at a time of growing demand and diminishing resources—and you get the picture. Overall, the cost of health care in America is rising faster than that of other goods and services. In fact, over the past forty years health care costs have risen an average of 2.4 percent faster than the national economy has grown. (See figure 6.) This increase is the primary reason that health care now represents approximately 17 percent of our economy, up from just 6.5 percent forty years ago. And this rapid rise is expected to continue. The only question is, at what rate?

Our government health care programs contribute enormously to this imbalance. The signature program for retirees, hospitalization insurance under Medicare, already pays out more in benefits than it takes in. Medicare as a whole had a financing gap of about $38 trillion as of January 1, 2009, which is about five times greater than Social Security's shortfall.

We need health care reform, we need it badly, and we need it soon. The problem is whether any given health care reform plan would make things better or worse. Americans want a better health care system. But we need a system we can afford and sustain. And we most certainly do not want Washington's bureaucracy, rather than our family doctors, to be in control of it.

Now it's President Obama's turn to come up with a workable formula. I'm not going to get into the ins and outs of any particular plan. The details and formulas are shifting daily as health care reform works its way through the legislative sausage factory. Suf-

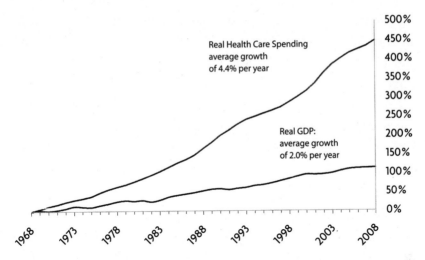

Figure 6 Cumulative growth in health care spending and GDP since 1968. Health care costs are growing faster than the economy.

fice it to say that President Obama favors universal health care coverage in a system where government-provided insurance (or a public option) is available but not mandatory. And, no surprise, he has been hazy about how we would pay for this coverage without borrowing even more and making our fiscal crisis even worse. One thing is clear: You can't reduce costs by expanding coverage.

It is also clear that the first priority of reform—making real progress on controlling costs—will require a new way of thinking about the problem. Yes, we need universal coverage, but first we need an honest discussion about what level of coverage is appropriate, affordable, and sustainable. To reform our health care system in a fiscally responsible way involves changing payment systems, reducing existing tax breaks, better targeting taxpayer premium subsidies for Medicare, pursuing integrated and alternative approaches to care, addressing difficult end-of-life issues, leveraging information technology, and reforming malpractice. Unfortunately, as of this writing, the health care reform plans being considered by the Congress do not address these issues in a meaningful way.

That includes the main issue—fiscal integrity. Given the Peterson Foundation's concern about this principle, we commissioned the Lewin Group to examine a major health care reform bill making its way through the House. The study found that the bill would cut the number of uninsured Americans by more than half, and the reform would almost pay for itself over the first ten years. But that's where the good news ended. For the ten years after that, the bill would add $1 trillion to projected federal deficits. In the end, we would have a health care system that was more expensive than the one we already have.

Thanks but no thanks. We need a system that pays for itself over the first ten years, does not add to federal deficits beyond ten years, and achieves a number of other key objectives. Let's hope President Obama meant it when he told a joint session of Congress: "I will not sign a plan that adds one dime to our deficits—either now or in the future. Period."

Has Congress agreed to a health care reform plan by the time you're reading this book? Does it improve our nation's financial condition, or dig our federal financial hole deeper? Does it address the tough issues, or did it punt on them? I'm betting that we have made some limited progress, in part as a tribute to Senator Ted Kennedy, but that the real tough choices it will take to reduce health care costs—yours, mine, and the federal government's—will not have been made. We all have to join this debate. Let this chapter be an issues guide that goes farther than the headlines you have been reading and efforts on both sides to spin the debate.

A HISTORY OF RISING COSTS

In the last chapter I wrote about some of the trends endangering Social Security. Well, our health care problem is not only more expensive than our Social Security problem, but much more extensive. This dilemma affects poor families, working families, and retirees alike.

Our health care crisis has been developing for decades. In our tradition of private enterprise, working Americans have counted on receiving health insurance at work. We have relied on employers to provide this insurance, to expand coverage, and to finance a large portion of overall health care costs. That system is best for taking care of workers in large companies that provide good insurance. But it has left tens of millions of Americans without any health insurance at all.

Those who do have insurance—and the employers who provide it—have become victims of cost run-ups. One major factor behind those soaring bills is that most of our personal health care costs are reimbursed on a fee-for-service basis. This means that providers are paid for what they do rather than for the results they achieve. This gives them a strong incentive, as in my wife's case, to do more in order to generate more revenue and reduce their litigation risk.

Our government health care programs are designed to absorb some of these costs—for some people. Like Social Security, they are intended as safety nets, in this case protecting poor and retired Americans. Medicaid, financed by the federal and state governments but administered by the states, helps poor people who cannot otherwise afford health care. Medicare, financed by the federal government, primarily serves people sixty-five years old and older, mainly retirees who typically have no other source of health insurance.

Medicare covers hospitalization, skilled nursing, hospice, and some home health services (Part A), and doctors' services, outpatient care, and some preventive services (Part B). It also includes an option for typical Medicare and possibly supplemental services to be provided through certain private plans (Part C), and it now offers some prescription drug coverage (Part D). The Medicare Part A program is funded with a payroll tax of 1.45 percent on all taxable wages and self-employment earnings. The tax is imposed both on workers and on their employers (for a total of 2.9 percent). Medicare Parts B, C, and D are voluntary programs that are funded in part by premiums paid by individuals who elect to join, partly by income tax revenues, and, in the case of Medicare Part D, partly by the states.

These programs comprise another huge portion of our nation's rising health care costs. About 83 million people, or 27 percent of our population, were insured through Medicare, Medicaid, and military health programs in 2007. In all, the federal government now pays about one-third of the nation's medical bills. As a result, Medicare and Medicaid have gone from approximately 4 percent of the federal budget in 1968 to about 20 percent in 2008. That percentage is still going up and will continue to climb as the baby boomers retire and our population ages.

Why have U.S. health care costs risen so rapidly? The fee-for-service excesses are part of the story. The boomers are part of the story. In addition, new medical technologies and procedures result in more advanced and more costly health care capabilities. Hospitals and specialists are racing to add them—and we have to pay for them. And here's another important factor: Our federal government runs the only major national health care system on Earth that does not have a budget (or limit) on what it spends. The U.S. government writes a blank check for health care.

There are many examples of how other countries provide services without going bankrupt. Germany, for one, allocates annual health care funding to cover its citizens in each major region of the country. The physicians and other health care professionals then decide whether certain services or procedures should be provided to a patient based on the individual's condition and on the related costs and potential benefits. And yes, this means not performing "heroic measures" (that is, procedures that may have little to no chance of meaningfully improving and extending life) at the end of life, irrespective of the patient's age. This financing approach recognizes that providing certain procedures, devices, or prescription drugs to one patient will limit the options for others.

In Sweden, the government also allocates a portion of its national budget to health care costs. If the actual costs go higher, then the premiums or taxes that individuals must pay automatically rise to offset the shortfall.

These are both ways to limit federal payments in a rational and responsible manner. But benefit payments are just part of the spiraling health care costs that our federal government faces. When it comes to health care, the government not only gives, it fails to receive. Here's why: Most people who benefit from employer-provided health insurance never have to pay income or payroll taxes on the value of the insurance provided by their employer. By fiscal 2008, these tax breaks cost the government about $288 billion a year in lost federal tax revenues, a loss that's growing steadily as health care gets more and more expensive. This also results in lost revenue at the state and local levels, since the value of employer-provided health insurance is also excluded from state and local income taxes.

Most people do not seem to understand how unfair these tax benefits are. Under this system, CEOs and other top earners in America, since they are in the highest tax brackets, receive more significant taxpayer subsidies than most of their employees do. And lower-income workers who do not have any employer-provided health insurance receive no taxpayer assistance. Under our tax system, the rich get generous subsidies, and those who do not qualify for Medicaid and aren't covered by an employer-sponsored plan have to fend for themselves. Does this seem right to you?

Even those individuals who have employer-provided health insurance and benefit from the related tax preferences are feeling the effects of higher health care costs. If you're a typical American and get health insurance on the job, you're probably paying a deductible that can top $1,000 a year, according to a recent study by Mercer Consultants—that's before your insurance even kicks in, and that's on top of any premiums and co-pays that you are responsible for.

That's expensive, but it could be much worse. If your employer does not give you insurance and you have to buy your own, you could be looking at an average annual cost of $21,000 to purchase comprehensive health insurance coverage for your family. How does that sound, when median household income in America is about $50,000 a year?

What we have here is a portrait of a system that is badly broken. Washington is having trouble paying the bills for our federal health care programs. At the same time, we consumers are having trouble covering our own medical costs. And many state and local governments also face large and growing deficits.

The states manage Medicaid health and long-term care benefits for the poor and are responsible for paying half of the program's spiraling costs. The states also have their own retiree health and pension plans to finance. Many are struggling to keep up with these costs while also maintaining critical infrastructure and state-sponsored education systems. Unlike our national government, states cannot print money, borrow without limit, or establish exotic trust funds. When state and local governments borrow and spend, they have to make the numbers work. In fact, all but one state have some sort of balanced budget requirement, although these vary in nature and effectiveness. In addition, states have to keep their finances in order to maintain a favorable credit rating.

Federal handouts are about the only relief states can hope for—and that's why many states lined up at the trough for federal help as part of the 2009 stimulus package and some, such as California, made later requests for federal assistance. Many states and localities are assuming that this aid pipeline from Washington will be a recurring fixture, but that is unrealistic.

How do we get out of this situation? That's the question the president and Congress are trying again to answer. Here's one way to assess the debate: Don't believe any politician who says that the government can expand health care coverage without eventually raising your taxes. Yes, there are plenty of opportunities to improve the efficiency of our health care system and eliminate the perverse incentives, but universal coverage, even for basic and essential services, will cost more money.

The fact is, the federal government has already promised way more than it can deliver. Of Medicare's approximately $38 trillion financing hole, about $7.2 trillion came from the new prescription drug benefit pushed through by Bush 43. And remember, many advocates claimed this program would save the federal government money!

Filling in our funding gap will be enormously painful. For example, to finance Medicare's hospitalization program (Part A) through 2083, the government would have to immediately raise the program's payroll tax from 2.9 percent to 6.78 percent or immediately cut the program's services by more than half. Imagine the outcry against any administration that made such a proposal. And that assumes that the annual increase in health care costs will be reduced to 1 percent in excess of annual economic growth within twenty-five years rather than the historical average of 2.4 percent.

Something has got to give. And yet some people want to give the government more responsibility for health care, without adequate financing. Take a look, for example, at the health care reform proposals that were working their way through Congress in the fall of 2009. Senate Finance Committee chairman Max Baucus (D-MT) produced a bill that would reduce federal deficits, according to the Congressional Budget Office—but only if implemented as designed. That was a big "if." The bill came under immediate attack from other Democrats, who complained that the Baucus formula imposed too great a financial burden on the middle class. They were sure to add amendments that would make the bill less fiscally responsible. Chairman Baucus's bill also relies on the willingness of Congress to make significant reductions in future provider reimbursement rates when it has consistently failed to do so in the past.

Given concerns regarding the doctor's reimbursement issue, in October 2009 Senate Majority Leader Harry Reid proposed to decouple this matter from overall health care reform, thereby potentially avoiding a need to pay for its $247 billion price tag. *The Washington Post* noted in an editorial that Mr. Reid's attempt to do so was "nonsensical." The *Post* also noted that some sort of "bipartisan commission" would be required to craft a "comprehensive solution."

The House of Representatives didn't help by voting to waive a 2010 premium increase for the Medicare plan that pays doctors' bills—irresponsibly cutting revenues at a time when Medicare already was heading deep into the red. This is just another example of fiscally irresponsible political pondering by elected officials.

Steps like these only serve to deepen our federal financial hole, increase our risk, and make our ultimate day of reckoning even more painful.

FALLING THROUGH THE CRACKS

As I discussed earlier, the near poor and people with lower-middle-class incomes often are not covered or are not adequately covered by insurance. They rely on emergency rooms when they need care, which is a tremendously costly, inefficient, and stressful way to treat them. Too often they can't pay the bill, leaving hospitals to absorb the losses and to bear most of the burden of treating uninsured people. This results in higher prices for those who can afford to pay, and in some cases hospitals must turn away people without insurance. It's hard to think of a more inefficient and cruel system of treating people.

The employers and government providers who have taken on the burden of many of these rising costs also are having trouble, especially in today's tough economic times. You can see this happening in the numbers. In 2000, 69 percent of all employers offered health insurance, according to the Kaiser Family Foundation's annual survey; by 2008, only 60 percent of employers were offering insurance—and only 45 percent of businesses with three to nine workers provided insurance. Given the current recession and other factors, the overall coverage rate is undoubtedly continuing to drop.

In 2007—before the recession hit us—roughly 45 million Americans under the age of sixty-five lacked health insurance. Two years later, that number was approaching 50 million and is now probably beyond that. Some of these people had the opportunity to purchase health care insurance through their employers but decided not to. Some were young people who didn't think they needed coverage, and others simply didn't think they could afford the premiums.

Still others had no choice: They lost their jobs. Under our current health care system, many unemployed Americans face a double whammy. Not only do they lose their employer-provided health insurance, but the state Medicaid programs designed to help the poor, facing financial pressures of their own, have cut back coverage. It's true that many laid-off workers can opt to continue their health care coverage for a time under federal law. Without an employer subsidy, however, they must pay the full price of that coverage.

Retirees too are losing coverage. Since health care costs are rising rapidly, employers have been either reducing or eliminating insurance for their former employees. In fact, less than 15 percent of American retirees now receive some form of employer-provided health care assistance.

THE QUALITY GAP

It is bad enough that our health care system costs too much and leaves too many people out. We also have to face the fact that the system itself is simply highly inefficient, and that directly affects the quality of the care we receive. Watchdogs have found plenty of evidence suggesting that we are not getting good value for our health care dollars. Studies show that quality is uneven across the nation, with many patients not receiving clinically proven, effective treatments. At the same time, many patients receive a range of unproven and ineffective treatments, because such treatments make the cash register ring and reduce litigation risk. And I'm talking about patients who are insured one way or another. People who aren't insured typically get shoddier treatment.

We Americans think of ourselves as world leaders—but not in the value, efficiency, and effectiveness of our overall health care system. Yes, we're number one in some health care statistics—including unfortunate measures such as cost per person. As I said earlier, we now spend about 17 percent of our nation's total annual economic production on health care, far more than other major industrialized countries spend. Yet all that money gets us below-average results in many areas. (See figure 7.)

Outcome	U.S. Ranking
Life Expectancy (77.8 years at birth in 2005)	25 out of 34
Infant Mortality (0.69% per live birth in 2005)	28 out of 33
Obesity (34% of those aged over 15 in 2006)	30 out of 30
Health Expenditure (15.3% of GDP in 2006)	30 out of 30

Figure 7 Health care outcomes among Organization for Economic Co-operation and Development (OECD) countries. We spend twice as much per person compared to other developed countries, and we have much worse outcomes. The system is badly broken.

There are a number of sad examples. For instance, we are number one in obesity. America's obesity rate has doubled in the past twenty years. More than three in ten Americans are now obese, by far the highest rate in the developed world. And obesity can be a leading indicator of diabetes, heart disease, and joint problems. Just ask my daughter-in-law Meghan, a nurse, how bad it can get. She needs the help of every other nurse on her hospital floor to get one five-hundred-pound patient out of bed several times a day.

Our infant mortality rate (6.9 per 1,000 live births) ranks among the worst of the thirty nations measured by the Organization for Economic Co-operation and Development (OECD). Our life expectancy at birth (77.8 years) is also below par.

When we do get sick or injured, our system has trouble making us feel better. The U.S. hospital infection rate is above average for an industrialized nation, a problem I have experienced firsthand. In 2007 I had to undergo a second surgery on my collarbone to address an infection from the first one.

The Commonwealth Fund, a private foundation that tracks health care performance, estimates that as many as 101,000 fewer Americans would die prematurely each year from treatable problems if the U.S. health care system performed as well as those in other leading industrial countries. According to the Commonwealth Fund's 2008 scorecard, the U.S. health care system is losing ground.

FOUR PILLARS OF REFORM

Reforming a health care system is especially difficult. After all, health care is about more than money. It is also about life and death. Health care reform is also vulnerable to manipulation by interest groups whose interest is in profit rather than effective health care. Without question, however, the United States' system needs more than a few tweaks. The problems I have outlined require comprehensive reform. The nature and scope of our reform program, along with the timing and financing, are critical issues that will determine whether we can achieve sustainable success. We need to make changes; however, if we get the basics wrong, we can make a bad system even worse.

Don't expect President Obama or anybody else to fix everything overnight. Reform should come in installments, not all at once. The reform effort will take courage, patience, persistence, perseverance, pain, and a degree of nonpartisanship that is hard to imagine. It will also require a difficult conversation about how to set priorities in a world of limited resources. But we can do it, and we can show results sooner rather than later if we go about it the right way.

Throughout this effort, we have to keep clear principles in mind. I see them as the four pillars of comprehensive health care reform.

My first pillar of reform should be financial discipline. We must impose a budget on what the federal government can spend on health care each year. As I will outline below, we should ultimately achieve universal coverage for "basic and essential" health care. But without a budget that limits the total amount of taxpayer funds allocated to health care costs, we will inevitably find our costs ballooning.

Financial discipline of this kind will be impossible as long as we have fee-for-service payment systems. There are several alternatives, among them, so-called capitation systems, in which providers take a flat fee to care for a patient or a group of patients each year. In general, we should also seek more of a team approach to providing patient care, integrating the services of hospitals, clinics, family doctors, therapists, specialists, pharmacists, and others. This includes taking steps to significantly reduce the rate of unnecessary hospital readmissions.

Another component of reducing costs will be medical malpractice reform. Obviously doctors have to be held accountable when they make mistakes. But a system in which juries award settlements involving millions of dollars without adequate expertise is not an appropriate way to deal with cases. The way around this is to appoint special courts to handle medical malpractice claims as we have for bankruptcies.

We can also encourage healthier lifestyles and generate additional revenues simultaneously. Why not adjust the health care premiums and coverage levels to discourage our fellow citizens who choose to smoke, for example? If you smoke, you might pay a higher premium and/or be subject to limitations on certain types of treatment.

The second pillar of reform is to impose better standards of practice. Americans love to try new vitamins and supplements, innovative treatments and therapies—anything that smacks of a fresh cure, especially if they think they won't have to pay for it. But our government cannot afford to pay for every pill that comes out of a box or every procedure known to man. As a matter of national policy, we must establish treatment standards based on sound clinical evidence of what works and what doesn't work. These standards must guide the practice of medicine and the dispensing of prescription drugs financed by taxpayer dollars.

Let me be very clear here. An American patient should have access to any treatments, technologies, and pills available, provided they are legal and the patient wants to pay for them. The key question is, what should the taxpayers finance? In my view, taxpayer-funded programs should pay only for treatments and medications that have proven clinical results, are cost effective, and would meaningfully improve or extend life.

We must employ more evidence-based practices to address the wide variance between geographic areas. These variances have been studied by researchers at Dartmouth and elsewhere, and they were the subject of a widely read article, "The Cost Conundrum," in *The New Yorker* in June 2009. Auther Atul Gawande examined a system in which Medicare reimbursements in impoverished McAllen, Texas, far exceeded those in Rochester, Minnesota, home of the high-tech, high-quality Mayo Clinic. Even President Obama said that he read the article.

Who should determine these evidence-based standards? The short answer is professionals, not politicians. We should set up a qualified and independent body of experts who have no current stake in the game—retired government health policy makers and former health industry executives, for example. This independent group could be our "health care Fed"—modeled after the Fed that supervises our money supply. The health care Fed would supervise our national health system, working to keep the standards vibrant and contemporary. A highly qualified panel of doctors, pharmacists, scientists, and specialists would advise the policy-making body.

The health care Fed would ultimately determine which medications, devices, and treatments are effective enough to be covered and which are not. The standards it developed would elevate the quality and consistency of American health care, prevent a lot of costly litigation, and save taxpayers the billions and billions of dollars each year they now spend on overpriced and ineffective treatments. The health care Fed could address tough coverage, reimbursement, and other decisions that politicians either won't or shouldn't make.

Let me add one other step we could take that would greatly raise our medical standards. The government should ban prescription drug advertising on television and possibly elsewhere. These ads create demand for expensive and often unnecessary products, and they should end.

The Supreme Court doesn't precisely agree with me. It has ruled that the pharmaceutical industry has a constitutional right to free speech and therefore to advertise. Nonetheless, Congress can impose a price for advertising pharmaceuticals. For example, it could make products that are advertised ineligible for certain federal drug programs, or it could make such advertising a nondeductible business expense on corporate income taxes.

Restricting advertising is just one of the reforms our pharmaceutical industry needs. Our government has to give it incentives to conduct the type of basic research that will actually improve our health. And Washington has to let cheaper imported drugs come to our stores—on a very selective basis—and also allow cheaper generic drugs to come to market faster.

My third pillar of health care reform is pretty basic. It's all of us. We have to take more individual responsibility for our own well-being.

This sounds like a no-brainer, but think of how a lot of us look at health care in our everyday lives. We go to the doctor when something is wrong. We go for the quick and easy route to good health—the crash diet or the magical pill. But that route is taking us in the wrong direction.

We have to build a culture of healthy living. While this is ultimately something that will come down to each of us as individuals, the government and particularly the schools can certainly play a role, as they did in campaigns to get us to wear seat belts or to recycle. This will have to be based on science, and of course there will be interest groups whose livelihoods will depend on throwing sand in the gears. Once again it will be up to us to make sure that any such campaign is transparent and carefully scrutinized.

Beyond that, we should practice the basics of well-being—eating nutritious food, taking vitamins, and getting adequate exercise—so consistently that these practices become a routine part of our lives. As my daughter-in-law Meghan says, just washing your hands frequently can make a big difference.

Finally, we must focus our efforts on achieving universal coverage for "basic and essential" health care. I put those words in quotes because we have to talk seriously about exactly what American taxpayers should fund. Our national health care system has to serve the basic needs of our society as a whole, not the un-limited wants of every individual. This system might be financed through the federal government, but fulfilled through private-sector providers. It may also make sense to change Medicare from its current design, over a long transition period, to a program that provides this basic and essential coverage for all legal residents.

Our "basic and essential" level of coverage should provide pre-ventive and wellness care, for example, including annual physicals and tests such as mammograms. It should also address chronic conditions while insuring us against the potentially ruinous costs of catastrophic accidents and illnesses. After all, health care costs are the number one cause of personal bankruptcies.

Beyond this national "basic and essential" program, individual Americans should be able to get further coverage as they think necessary, provided they are willing to pay for it. The poor and in-digent still will have Medicaid. And everybody will have the right to buy supplemental insurance from a competitive pool of providers—through employers, unions, industry associations, pro-fessional and trade groups, and regional and nongovernmental co-operatives. Private plans should be able to be offered across state lines. They should provide for enhanced portability of benefits, not exclude preexisting conditions, and not contain unreasonable lim-its on coverage. The federal government might also provide an op-tion, but the plan must be market-based and not receive extra taxpayer subsidies; otherwise, we will likely end up with another unaffordable and unsustainable federal program—only much bigger—than the ones we have today.

Although other countries' programs have been used mostly as a way to frighten people away from reform, we can in fact learn a lot from their experiences, as well as those of the states, many of which are miles ahead of the federal government in providing effi-cient care. For example, Washington State has a very successful co-operative plan. Oregon has prioritized what procedures it will pay for under Medicaid. Massachusetts has moved to provide its residents with universal coverage, though its legislature is struggling to contain costs and provide optimum service.

We can supplement this culture of well-being with a national program that works to keep us healthy, helps pay for catastrophic costs, treats us according to evidence-based standards, offers supplemental insurance, and doesn't break the bank or burden future generations. Over the next generation, these principles can reshape American health care, public and private—including Medicare and Medicaid.

HOW TO REFORM MEDICARE

Some people say we should focus on achieving comprehensive health care reform now and worry about Medicare and Medicaid later. But these programs are hemorrhaging money, if you'll excuse the analogy, and need immediate treatment. There are three tough but necessary steps we could take right now to stanch the losses and bring in more revenue.

Our government could start by negotiating more aggressively on behalf of benefit recipients and requiring more competitive bidding for Medicare and Medicaid and other federal health programs. If the Veterans Administration can negotiate for better prescription drug prices for veterans, we should be able to do so for drugs as well as other products and services in federal health care programs for nonveterans.

Next, we could cut costs out of the Medicare Advantage program, also known as Part C. It was created to provide more alternatives and to encourage competition by providing more benefit choices and various options through competing private plans. It was supposed to save taxpayers money. But in actuality, it is costing taxpayers more money on a risk-adjusted basis. People who are covered under these plans tend to be healthier than the typical American senior.

Finally, there's a commonsense way to bring in more revenue.

Medicare should charge more to those of us who can afford to pay more. We pay for Medicare Part A (hospitalization insurance) through payroll taxes during our working lives. But Medicare Part B (doctor payments) and Part D (prescription drug benefits) are voluntary. If we want them, we have to pay a premium to get them. A vast majority of eligible Americans do so because they get such a great deal. Why? Because under present law, on average, the taxpayers subsidize about 75 percent of the real cost of these programs.

A government subsidy may be fine for a retiree who scrapes by just above the poverty level and is not eligible for Medicaid. But it makes no sense for middle- and upper-income recipients. It makes even less sense now that we are running large and growing deficits.

In addition to taking these specific steps, we need Medicare and other federal health care programs to lead the reform effort by example. This leadership would include, for example, requiring that the results of any major federal investments in health information technology, evidence-based medicine, and other areas are incorporated into Medicare's payment system. Health care providers would be required to use them—or face economic penalties if they did not.

The failure of Washington to use taxpayer dollars wisely has led to unsustainable health care programs that benefit the rich as much as the poor. If these programs were redesigned and properly administered, they would better serve those who are less well-off, and they could meet the basic and essential needs of all Americans.

OBAMA'S REFORMS

As I write this, the pressure is on the Obama administration to do something. Underinsured Americans and their underfinanced local and state governments are all looking to Washington for a way out of this national health care mess.

The political debate has become as frenzied as it was the last time a Democratic president proposed a major health care reform. President Clinton's attempt in the early 1990s, led by First Lady Hillary Clinton, failed to make it far in Congress. That effort was brought down in part by the very effective "Harry and Louise" ads, sponsored by insurers, showing a middle-class couple despairing over the bureaucratic complexities of Clinton's plan. Now we have Obama's opponents charging that he will convene "death panels" to grant or withhold treatment for gravely ill Americans. This is a gross misrepresentation of the legislative proposals and amounts to nothing more than a scare tactic.

The truth is, Obama's proposals at most would add a federal health insurance program only as an alternative to the private system we already have. We could all keep our family doctors and avoid bureaucrats, staying far from the reach of any "death panel."

Ignore all that political noise. Obama's commitment to comprehensive health care reform is a good sign. It puts him ahead of his predecessor in this regard. But will he make sure that his proposals are fiscally responsible and sustainable—and not just for ten years? A study commissioned by the Peterson Foundation has shown that while many of the health care reform proposals being considered by the Congress don't pay for themselves even over ten years, the financing gap worsens beyond the ten-year time frame. In the final analysis, any effort to expand coverage without transformational reforms that significantly shrink the federal financial hole and seriously reduce the rate at which our total costs as a percentage of the economy are growing would be imprudent.

My greatest fear is that the Obama administration and Congress will enact universal health care coverage without making a significant down payment on the $38 trillion of unfunded Medicare benefits that we already have, and without ensuring that the plan will actually contain total health care costs. Yes, we need comprehensive health care reform. However, any such reform should help us get out of our fiscal mess while improving the equity and outcomes of today's system. Those goals are not always so obvious in the wonderland of Washington.

We must avoid any temptation to add a new wing onto our existing health care house (system), which is already structurally unsound and headed for foreclosure. That is what some are proposing in Washington, and it's not only imprudent, it's irresponsible.

Our nation got into deep trouble by promising more health care than it could deliver. That approach has given Americans one of the most expensive systems in the world with among the least impressive results. My greatest hope is that we have begun to understand the predicament we are in and will come together to fix the system.

The outline of a reform program is clear. The hard part is finding politicians who have the courage to make the tough choices, resist the sweet siren songs of lobbyists, and do what is right for our country rather than for their careers. They need to make tough choices and stick to them even though the right choice may not be popular. After all, that is what true leadership is all about.

If we can find good leaders, transform our health care system, and adequately finance it, we will have come a long way toward creating a more promising fiscal future. That takes me to the next important issue we have to figure out together: revenues. On to the next chapter, and a topic you've been waiting for—our tax system!

Seven

COLLECT MORE REVENUE—MORE FAIRLY

Who likes taxes? I don't, and I would bet that you don't either. We can agree on that, though I'll have to work hard to make you agree on a few other things in this chapter.

The past fifty years have seen a reduction in federal income tax rates, but it would be a mistake to conclude that this makes us a low-tax society. In some combination or other, we pay federal income and payroll taxes (e.g., for Social Security and Medicare), state income and sales taxes, and local sales and property taxes. To complete the list of what we give to various governments, you would have to toss a number of other payments in the pot—excise taxes, tariffs, duties, fees, premiums, and so on. Think about that cable/phone/Internet bill that was supposed to be $99 per month. By the time you get done with all of the added fees, the bill has gone up by 10 percent or more. And let's face it, we indirectly pay corporate taxes, too, to the extent companies raise prices to offset them.

And so it feels as if we're getting hit with a tax everywhere we turn, which is somewhat ironic for a country that since its founding has shown a marked distrust for government's ability to tax us honestly. Today's system, complex and opaque as it is, heightens that mistrust. Instead of charging us fairly for services rendered, the federal government seems to be trying to confuse us and trick us out of money. They don't really care if we don't understand how and why we're being taxed. They just want us to fill out the forms and fork over more money. Since we can't even be sure we've prepared the forms correctly, we naturally suspect that we've ended up paying too much.

But it's my job to tell it to you straight, and here it is: In the aggregate, we actually aren't paying enough. As I pounded home in earlier chapters, we are not even close to paying for what government spends today, much less what it has promised for tomorrow—and this shortfall is growing dramatically.

I'm talking about our federal tax policies when I say that. State and local governments are generally required by law or their constitutions to balance their budgets. But the federal government is not, and takes full advantage of that huge loophole.

The freedom to spend money they don't have allows our leaders in Washington to play all kinds of con games. Their biggest lie is when they keep on spending but tell us they have "cut" taxes (Washington word alert). They haven't cut them at all. They have just borrowed the money and deferred the taxes to later generations, with interest—to Americans who are too young to vote and may not have been born yet. It's the worst kind of buy now, pay later plan. It's also a massive form of taxation without representation.

As I started writing this chapter, in April 2009, I was both gathering information for my own returns and reviewing reports of the antitax "Tea Party" demonstrations taking to the streets around the country. April 15 is always a great day for tax protests, but at this point in our history those tea parties looked out of place. On

April 15, 2009, Americans actually were paying less in total taxes than most other people in the industrialized world and, thanks to the Bush cuts, less than we recently had been. All those demonstrators gave cable TV something to cover, but they had little basis for complaining about today's overall federal tax levels. At the same time, they had plenty to complain about with regard to out-of-control spending.

We have to stop lying to ourselves. To get our fiscal house in order, we have to fix not only our system for spending money, but our system for bringing it in. In other words, tax reform is a key element of our efforts to restore our nation's financial health.

You're not going to like this, but we need more revenues, and more ways of collecting them, not fewer—and I'm going to propose a new kind of tax later in the chapter. Just know at the start that what I suggest will be a lot simpler, fairer, and more competitive than what we have now.

OUR SYSTEM IS TOO COMPLEX

I usually prepare my taxes myself, without help from an accountant or one of those programs designed to help you complete the forms. During my tenure as comptroller general, I urged senior members of the executive and legislative branches, including elected officials, to do the same. It's the best way I've found to show the powers that be how desperately our tax system needs reform. Unfortunately, people didn't generally take up my suggestion, not even the chairmen of the tax-writing committees in the Congress. When I proposed it to then Senate Finance Committee chairman Chuck Grassley (R-IA), his answer was short and sweet: "I do not accept the challenge."

I can't say I entirely blame him. Today, we have a system that is so mind-numbingly complex that it's almost impossible for the average taxpayer to comply with the law.

If you have any itemized deductions at all, just try wading

through all the various forms and schedules that the IRS now requires. Form 1040 started out as four pages in 1913 (too long even then!), and now it can grow to the size of a fashion magazine before you're through making all the calculations and documenting your financial life. You can read every dense line of instructions and still not be sure you've arrived at the correct figure for taxes due.

If the forms themselves are not bad enough, the Internal Revenue Code that they are based on has grown to encyclopedic size. Today's Internal Revenue Code is over 3,500 pages in length, up from fifteen in 1913. Add to the pages in today's code the thousands of additional pages and other guidance issued by the IRS. The code is so complex primarily because it outlines what is and what isn't taxable, at what times, in what amounts, and at what rates. This is even more difficult than you may think, because our tax law includes so many special tax preferences, otherwise known as loopholes, that people and businesses may be eligible for.

OUR SYSTEM IS UNFAIR

Tax preferences take many forms. They involve deductions, exemptions, exclusions, accelerations, credits, and carryovers, just to name a few. Is your head spinning yet? All of these provisions are the result of the executive branch or the Congress—or somebody—attempting to promote certain types of behavior. Maybe it was fashionable at one time to promote home ownership, savings, research and development, or employer-provided health care—you can find breaks for all of these things in the tax code. Then there are the breaks for certain farmers, insurers, contractors, and a long list of special interests—that is, just about anybody with influence in Washington and enough money to hire an imaginative lawyer and effective lobbyist.

All these preferences serve to complicate the tax code and reduce revenue so much that our basic tax rates are higher than they might otherwise be. Believe it or not, the federal government loses over $1 trillion in revenue a year due to these tax preferences.

The largest tax breaks might surprise you—or even benefit you. (See figure 8.) Coming in at number one in annual losses, with about $288 billion in 2008, is health insurance—that is, the income taxes and payroll taxes that most Americans *do not* pay on employer-provided health insurance. This preference subsidizes the health care of well-paid individuals who have high marginal tax rates, but, as I previously noted, it doesn't provide a dime of help for near-poor workers who lack employer-provided health insurance. This preference also encourages eligible workers to load up on health insurance simply to take advantage of the special tax breaks that come with these benefits. Shouldn't this tax preference at least be limited to the cost of a reasonable level of coverage?

The second-biggest tax break comes from the variety of savings incentives in the Internal Revenue Code. There are many, and they total over $120 billion in annual losses. While we want to promote

Exclusion for health care (income and payroll)	$288 billion
Exclusion for retirement income plans (IRAs, 401(k)s, defined benefits, etc.)	$120 billion
Exclusion of state and local taxes (income and property)	$74 billion
Exclusion of mortgage interest rate deductions	$67 billion
Exclusion of charitable contributions	$47 billion
TOTAL	**$596 billion**

Figure 8 Value of selected tax preferences, 2008. These tax preferences cost a lot of money, but, in many cases, they benefit the wealthy rather than the middle and lower income classes.

savings, as I have already shown you, our tax incentives don't work. After all those breaks, we still have the lowest savings of any major industrialized nation.

The third-biggest tax preference is the state and local tax deduction, which you get unless you pay the Alternative Minimum Tax (AMT), like I do. That amounts to $74 billion in annual losses.

Coming in at number four is the $67 billion in annual losses from the home mortgage interest deduction. You can argue that the deduction is appropriate since, to some, home ownership is the American Dream. At the same time, shouldn't there be more reasonable and regional limits on the size of a mortgage that qualifies for a deduction? For example, you could peg the deduction to the maximum conforming loan offered by one of the federal mortgage companies (Fannie Mae or Freddie Mac), an amount that varies by geographic area.

I could go on and on listing tax preferences, and they would get more and more obscure. Do you and I take full advantage of them? Do some of us take too much advantage of them? I was the chief auditor of the U.S. government for almost ten years and I've been a CPA for decades. But can I say my hand-prepared tax returns were correctly calculated every year? Well, I believe they were, and I can assure you that I completed them to the best of my knowledge—and with plenty of frustration.

I don't know about yours, but around the Walker household, tax preparation day is the worst time of the year. Mary is in charge of collecting receipts and forms, and I'm in charge of calculations and paperwork. The process never works—how shall I put it?—tranquilly. Something's always missing; something's always mixed up. In all, it's just not a very pleasant experience for either of us, and I don't think we're the only American family that would admit that.

In 2009 I took a break. I'll admit that I had a CPA firm do my 2008 taxes. That year I was based part of the time in D.C. and part of the time in New York. My primary residence was in Mt. Vernon, Virginia, yet I traveled all over the country. As a result, I had to apportion my income for state tax purposes. To put it simply, I needed help figuring out which tax collectors were due what based on the various state residency laws and other tax rules. However, in 2010 I plan to pick up the pencil and do my own taxes again. And, as always, it won't be a pleasant experience.

THE PATH TO TAX REFORM

If we Americans simply paid the taxes we owed, it wouldn't come close to solving our fiscal problems, but it would make a dent. In the fiscal year ending September 30, 2008, for example, the federal government collected $2.6 trillion in revenue, at least $300 billion short (based on a 2001 IRS estimate) of what should have been paid. This is the so-called tax gap. In some cases, the nonpayment was the result of mistakes; in some, it was illegal evasion. All in all, that's not a bad record when you consider that Americans report their income and pay their taxes voluntarily, with limited real enforcement by the government.

All the same, the tax gap between what should be paid and what actually is paid creates inequities. It means that the most honest Americans are subsidizing those who aren't. While $300 billion might be a fairly low percentage of federal receipts, it's still a lot of money. Don't let the trillion-dollar-plus annual deficits make you think otherwise.

We've reformed the tax system before. Most recently, in 1986, President Reagan signed a law that reduced our top tax rate on individual income from 50 percent to 28 percent. There was a higher 33 percent rate that simply ensured that higher-income taxpayers paid 28 percent on all their taxable income. That law also cut tax loopholes and preferences, most notably those related to interest payments in credit card loans and a number of real estate tax shelters. It also raised business taxes. All of these changes were designed to allow the IRS to collect roughly the same amount of money despite lower marginal tax rates.

Since then, not surprisingly, the top individual rate has crept back up to 35 percent. In addition, many preferences made their way back into the code between 1986 and 2008, and with them, another seven hundred pages. Yes, our tax system is probably more complex these days than it was before 1986, and it's getting bigger and more complex every year.

Now we have to go back to basics again. The least we can do is simplify the tax system according to the Reagan model: Keep the rates as low as possible, broaden the tax base by cutting preferences, and make the rules easier for us to comply with and for the IRS to enforce.

I know, I know. You hear calls for tax reform all the time. Every new administration comes to office promising it. President Obama ordered his economic advisers to come up with a simpler tax system by the end of his first year. Former Fed chairman Paul Volcker is heading a group to make related recommendations. He is extremely capable and credible, so I look forward to seeing what they come up with. Unfortunately, President Obama has complicated things by promising tax cuts to middle-class Americans and special tax breaks to small businesspeople, students, first-time home buyers, and others. He also said that he would never raise taxes for individuals making less than $250,000 a year. If you believe that, then you are very gullible, because the math doesn't come close to working if President Obama means what he says about fiscal responsibility.

There is nothing unusual about Obama's approach. American presidents almost from the start have had to tax and give tax relief simultaneously—a task all the more challenging as demands on government services have increased. President Lincoln imposed the first U.S. income tax in 1862 to help pay for the Civil War. That levy was repealed a decade later, and in 1895 the Supreme Court struck down Congress's attempt to revive it.

COLLECT MORE REVENUE—MORE FAIRLY

The income tax returned in 1913 as a result of the Sixteenth Amendment to the U.S. Constitution, which allowed Congress to collect the tax without apportioning the revenue among the states. It's been with us ever since and probably always will be. It was supplemented by the Social Security payroll tax beginning in 1935 and the Medicare payroll tax in 1965.

That 1913 law levied a 1 percent tax on net personal incomes above $3,000. There was an exception: If you made more than $500,000, you paid a 6 percent surtax. This was controversial at the time but seems modest compared to current tax rates—and so simple. By the way, $3,000 and $500,000 in 1913 are equal to about $65,000 and $11,000,000, respectively, in 2009. Under the federal tax system of 1913, I would pay only 1 percent of my income to the federal government. Instead, even though I'm not a wealthy person, I paid almost 30 percent of my income to the federal government alone in 2008, and that excludes the employer portion of Social Security and Medicare taxes. It also excludes state and local taxes.

Over the years, the income tax system has become more complex, and tax rates have risen to pay for wars and finance the growing size of the federal government. For example, in 1916 the lowest rate was raised to 2 percent and the top rate was raised to 15 percent for taxpayers with incomes in excess of $1.5 million (in 1916 dollars). The Social Security tax was added in 1935. Income tax rates rose again in 1941. Tax cuts followed after World War II, but the tax system got more complex and rates rose over time until the Reagan era. The Medicare tax was added in 1965. Major tax reform was achieved in 1986, but again the code has grown more complex and rates have risen since then.

So how do we reform this system? This is a particular challenge, given our historical antipathy to taxes of any kind. But Americans believe in fairness, and I think a reform that emphasized making the system fairer by ending preferences would capture widespread support. However, any major tax reform campaign will have to be part of a much broader government transformation effort that engages citizens in new and unprecedented ways. And any effort designed to raise more federal tax revenues will need to be coupled with major entitlement reforms and statutory spending controls.

MAKE THE SYSTEM SIMPLER

The Internal Revenue Service has been working to crack down on tax cheats while improving its technology and efficiency. But a system like ours, with so many preferences and so much paperwork, is still way too complex. To really close the tax gap, we will have to streamline and simplify the entire tax code. Again emphasizing the idea of fairness, we should support tax enforcers by giving them more information about transactions in our economy—such as how much money investors make (or lose) when they buy stocks, among other things. We should also have tax withheld automatically from payments to independent contractors, partners in professional services firms, and others who now make their own estimated tax payments. If you work for a company, you have taxes withheld automatically from your paycheck. Why shouldn't the same thing happen if you work as a contractor or partner in a professional services firm?

Similarly, we should take another look at the tax breaks we allow for health care. In any reform leading to national health insurance, the government's role might be to provide a safety net for all legal residents, to promote wellness and preventive care, and to protect us against catastrophic medical expenses. But suppose the cost of such a government health plan is $5,000 a year and our employer gives us comprehensive coverage costing $12,000 a year. Why shouldn't we pay taxes on that extra $7,000 of health care coverage?

We could take another huge step toward a simpler tax system by getting rid of the con game known as the Alternative Minimum

Tax. The AMT dates back to 1969, when Congress decided to go after rich Americans who claimed so many deductions that they ended up paying little or no income tax. The problem is that the income levels that triggered the AMT were not indexed for inflation—which means that as inflation has raised salaries, millions of middle-income taxpayers have been hooked into paying the AMT. Maybe their incomes would have made them rich in 1969, but they aren't rich today, especially if they live in New York City or other very expensive metropolitan areas.

These AMT victims dutifully fill out their tax forms, taking normal deductions for state taxes, dependents, and so on—then discover that it was all no more than a pencil exercise because under AMT rules their deductions disappear and they owe much more. The government has just played a bait-and-switch game with them. Now you see your deductions, and now you don't. Surprise! I can think of different language, but I won't use it here.

We should do away with this complicated and unseemly exercise in taxpayer deception—or at least reform the AMT so that it applies only to the country's richest households, as it was originally intended to do.

Congress won't take such steps lightly; cutting the AMT would cost at least $800 billion in revenues over ten years, a loss that might require our legislators to raise tax rates. But our government should tax us honestly rather than conning us out of our money and making us waste a lot of time filling out forms that don't really matter. I must tell you that I have paid the AMT four out of the past five years. To me, it is nothing more than a dishonest surtax—a surtax that resulted in me paying about 18 percent more in federal income taxes in 2008, and I'm not a wealthy person. This is one case where it would be better to raise rates than perpetuate the deception on nonwealthy taxpayers.

The reality is, under the AMT, the only itemized deductions that individuals really get are for charitable contributions and for mortgage interest on a primary residence. As of this writing, I don't have such a mortgage, since I practice what I preach—minimizing debt and maximizing savings. I had a mortgage until ten years ago, when paying mine off helped me afford to return to government service.

MAKE THE SYSTEM FAIRER, TOO

A streamlined tax system would be easier to comply with and easier to enforce. More Americans would pay the taxes they owe. But we also have to broaden the tax base so that more of us share the cost of financing the government we want. You've heard that old expression: "Don't tax you, don't tax me, tax the guy behind the tree." Well, forget it. Today, as Pete Peterson says, it's more like, "Don't tax you, don't tax me, tax the baby on your knee."

In a nutshell, we have to extend the reach of our income tax system and make it fairer. We have to keep payroll tax rates as low as we can but still deliver on the promises we have made for Social Security and Medicare. And if we can't generate enough revenue from these traditional sources, we have to consider another source—some kind of national consumption tax, possibly earmarked to pay for the universal basic and essential health care plan I've discussed.

Right now, our system is anything but fair and balanced. After the Bush 43 tax cuts, two-thirds of all working Americans paid more in payroll taxes—which finance Social Security and Medicare—than in income taxes. In addition, more than 40 percent of Americans pay no income taxes at all. That is, they pay nothing to finance just about every other federal expenditure, including all of the express and enumerated functions envisioned for the federal government by our Founding Fathers. Obama's tax proposals would make the percentage of freeloaders even larger. Under his changes, as many as half of all working Americans would pay only payroll taxes. Think of that: Over half of all working Americans would probably end up paying no income tax at all!

What does this trend mean? For one thing, we have to become more holistic in our thinking. When we talk about the federal tax burden, we can't just consider income taxes; we have to think about the combination of income and payroll taxes.

When you look at the combined tax burden, you get a very different picture of the distribution of taxes. (See figure 9.) What you see is that the top 20 percent of taxpayers pay about 69 percent of the total of all income and payroll taxes. What you don't see is that payroll taxes are inadequate to keep Social Security and Medicare

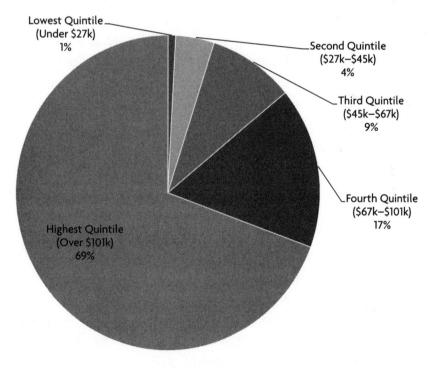

Figure 9 Who pays what in taxes (2006 tax year). The graph shows where the money raised through federal payroll and income taxes comes from. For instance, just 1 percent of the revenue comes from the poorest 20 percent of the population. The top 40 percent of households pay about 86 percent of all federal payroll and income taxes. (The income ranges are the combined annual pretax income of a two-person household.)

afloat. In addition, fewer people are paying for bedrock govern-ment programs like defense, homeland security, foreign relations, the federal judicial system, our national infrastructure, environ-mental protection, and the like. All of these programs are funded via the income tax. Do we want a tax system in which most of us don't pay for national defense and homeland security? I don't.

We need to distribute our taxpaying burden more equitably. We should ensure that all Americans except the poorest pay some min-imum level of income tax—say, 10 percent of the amount of in-come above a geographically adjusted level.

This is where my proposal for a new consumption tax comes in. I can hear you screaming, but let me reemphasize a major point of this book: There are only two kinds of taxes, the ones we pay now and the ones we pay later or defer to our children and grand-children, with interest. I say we take on our responsibilities as cit-izens now, cleaning up our deficits and debts when the costs are cheaper than they will be if we pawn them off on our kids. As George Washington said, "We should avoid ungenerously throw-ing upon posterity the burdens that we ourselves ought to bear." These are timeless words of wisdom that today's elected officials should heed.

Let's put things in perspective. Americans pay less in taxes than people do in other major developed countries. In 2007, taxes at all levels of government represented nearly 28 percent of our econ-omy, compared with an average of 37 percent in the Organization for Economic Co-operation and Development (OECD), the club of major market economies. Among the thirty members of that global club, only Mexico, Japan, Korea, and Turkey had lower overall tax burdens than the United States.

If we do nothing at all, our taxes will rise in the near future. Bush 43's tax cuts all were enacted temporarily and are set to ex-pire at the end of 2010. Our elected officials need to decide which of those tax cuts to retain, which should be modified, and which should be allowed to expire. If they all expire, that would raise our federal tax rate from its historical level—about 18.3 percent of the economy over the last four decades—to 24 percent by 2050 and rising. That won't happen, since there is bipartisan support to extend the middle-class and selected other Bush tax cuts.

Americans are not likely to support a 24 percent and rising overall federal tax burden without another real Tea Party. Yet that level is still not enough to pay the federal government's bills. At the same time, total federal tax burdens could be less than this if we start to make tough choices. So we need to act sooner rather than later to impose long-overdue statutory budget controls, entitlement and tax reforms, and other changes necessary to keep future taxes at a reasonable level. The truth is, the longer we wait to institute tough budget control, reform entitlement programs, and make tax changes, the higher taxes are likely to go up over time. Timely action can get the power of compounding to work for us rather than against us, as it is now.

TAXING CONSUMPTION

Consumption taxes, especially progressive ones, make sense because they spread the burden of taxation and encourage saving. We already have some forms of consumption tax; for example, state sales taxes and federal excise taxes on items like gasoline and guns. I am for consumption taxes as long as the essentials of life (basic foodstuffs, clothing, shelter) are exempt or otherwise recognized. Until now the United States has shied away from the widespread use of consumption taxes because they can serve to penalize poor people, taking a relatively bigger bite out of their financial resources. The rest of the world has not been so shy. The OECD countries take more than 30 percent of their tax revenue on average from consumption taxes; the United States takes less than 10 percent, ranking at the bottom of that list.

One particular consumption tax is more popular than all the others around the world. In the past half century, more than a hundred countries have adopted a value-added tax (VAT), a form of indirect sales tax. Every OECD country—except the United States—has a VAT.

The VAT doesn't hit just consumers at the point of final sale, like other sales taxes. Rather, it is imposed at every stage in the production process that adds value—for example, when a tree becomes a plank of wood, when the wood becomes a chair, when the chair is sold wholesale, and finally when it's sold retail. Businesses with long production chains are not penalized because they pay taxes only on the value added in their transaction and can take credits on earlier taxes along the chain. Governments can allow for other credits or rebates as they see fit—to certain industries, say, or to low-income citizens, or to tourists. If you've had your VAT refunded at a European airport, you know how this system works.

In my ideal world, we would get rid of our income tax system with all of its complications and rely on consumption taxes for a significant share of federal revenues. The VAT is easy to administer, deducted automatically in every transaction. (According to some, we might be able to get rid of the IRS!) Policy makers can favor certain industries and taxpayers simply by adjusting the relevant rates and credits. (No more squadrons of lawyers finding loopholes!) Finally, a consumption tax encourages savings over conspicuous consumption: You can dodge taxes only by being more careful about how you spend your money. It is also a way to tax very wealthy people without having to distinguish between their accumulated wealth and their current income. Their tax shelters would no longer save them from taxes.

Okay, time to stop dreaming. Some version of Form 1040 and April 15 will probably continue to be aspects of the American nightmare for many years to come. But let's at least include a national consumption tax as part of an efficient, fair new system to generate the revenues we need to close the deficit, reduce our debt, and address other key national priorities. We need more money to pay our bills, and adding a new tax, after we enact tough new statutory budget controls and spending limits, may make sense as an alternative to dramatically raising our income and payroll tax rates and putting more pressure on an already creaky foundation of our tax policy.

And what about the estate tax? In my view, it should not be repealed but the exclusion limit should be raised and indexed for inflation, and the tax rate should be held at a reasonable level. Why not repeal it? Because, can you imagine how wealth would be further concentrated in this country over time? My Walker family line has never had enough money to worry about the estate tax, but I know many other families that have. The truth is, many people who benefit from second- and third-generation inherited wealth do not necessarily use it wisely.

LET'S BE WORLD WISE

You'll note that my argument considers our national tax system in the context of the rest of the world. Some Americans—including many of those "Tea Party" protesters—don't buy that approach. They argue that the rest of the world doesn't count: America has to stay true to its own culture of taxing and spending.

It's not that simple in an increasingly interconnected and interdependent world. Many countries have higher taxes than ours because they finance national health insurance. Does that give their workers more flexibility and mobility than ours, who always have to worry about health care before switching jobs? Does it help their economies ride out downturns better than ours, where a worker can suffer a catastrophic loss of job and health coverage simultaneously? We should consider questions like these, which tell us a lot about our domestic compassion and global competitiveness.

What about corporate taxes? Right now, the U.S. corporate tax rate is more than 12 percent higher than the OECD average. In fairness, there are numerous special tax preferences accorded to U.S. corporations that serve to reduce the rate that many major corporations pay. In fact, many corporations pay little to no income taxes as a result of these special tax provisions. Furthermore, there are a number of special deferral arrangements and other deals that apply to multinational corporations. These are very complex and very difficult for the IRS to enforce. The truth is, the IRS is largely outgunned and out-resourced when it comes to corporate tax compliance, especially when it has to deal with very large multinational corporations.

If we are going to have corporate taxes, which should be debated, we need to make sure that our corporate tax structure is appropriate to the times. For starters, U.S. corporations work for their shareholders, not for the American common good, and will use their considerable legal brainpower to avoid taxes wherever they can. Once again, simplicity is our best tool. We need to broaden the base of corporate taxation, keep the tax rates low, and minimize the number of deductions, credits, and exclusions that the corporate lawyers can use to reduce their companies' effective tax rates.

It's also important that our corporate tax structure should help improve our competitive position abroad. For example, the United States taxes income earned abroad at much higher rates than most countries do. These rules make dodging U.S. taxes almost a competitive necessity for our multinationals—and cry out for a simpler system featuring lower rates and a broader base of taxable income.

Please keep two important principles in mind. While most Americans have no desire to move anywhere else, corporations will if the tax laws or regulatory structures become too onerous.

At the same time, we must realize that corporations don't really pay taxes. Rather, they pass along any tax, in the form of higher prices to consumers, lower wages to workers, and/or lower returns to shareholders.

THE REFORM DEBATE

The changes I'm suggesting in this chapter fit the principles I've kept in mind throughout this book. They respect our values, make best use of our financial resources, and are fairer for the next generation. They also make common sense. If we want to raise tax money the American way, we have to keep the rates low and make sure we all pay our fair share.

There are, of course, many other voices in the debate. Let's not spend much time on the voices from the fringes, such as those that argue for either a welfare state or tax-free capitalism. Keep in mind, contrary to assertions by some, not all tax cuts stimulate the economy, and very few tax cuts pay for themselves. To pay for themselves, they have to result in more gross tax revenue after the tax cut than would have been received without the tax cut.

Others have more dramatic proposals for transforming our tax system. Former House majority leader Dick Armey (R-TX) has long advocated a "flat tax." Under this approach, the tax base would be broadened and all taxpayers would pay a single tax rate on all taxable income above a stated level. Wages would continue to be subject to Social Security and Medicare payroll taxes.

An even more dramatic tax reform approach has been advocated by Representative John Linder (R-GA) and others. Under their "fair tax" proposal, all individual and corporate income and payroll taxes would be repealed and replaced with a national consumption-based tax of about 30 percent on all purchases of goods and services. All individuals would receive a tax credit for purchases up to a stated level (for example, $10,400 for one person and $21,200 for a family of four in the continental United States). This approach would attempt to preserve the benefits of a consumption tax while avoiding its impact on our less-well-off fellow citizens. A side benefit of this approach, some assert, would be the elimination of the IRS—although some federal entity would need to manage the new system of credits. Irrespective of the intellectual merits of this system, the political feasibility is highly questionable.

The fairness of any new federal system would have to be judged by how equitably the burdens are shared by Americans rich and poor. We must also be concerned with the adequacy of our tax system. In the final analysis, it must generate enough revenues to pay our bills and deliver on the promises that the federal government intends to keep.

By now you recognize my mantra. The expansion of government over time, excessive spending, and the continuing cry for tax relief have been driving us toward bankruptcy. What we need is tax reform: a simpler, fairer, more transparent, and user-friendly system that brings sufficient revenues into our Treasury and uses them more productively—not to finance more unaffordable and unsustainable wants, but to meet essential needs for America and Americans. I have outlined some of these reforms in this chapter. These reforms not only will assist in our pursuit of happiness, they will boost America's competitiveness in the global economy.

It's time to look more closely at our place in the global economy. Our international trade and financial policies have something in common with the domestic issues I've been talking about up to this point: They are in disarray. We have become increasingly enamored with imports and reliant on foreign lenders. These trends, if not reversed, risk weakening our foreign policy, threatening our national security, and even harming our domestic tranquility over time. I'll show you how in the next chapter and explain how we can improve our international standing.

Eight

ADDRESSING AMERICA'S INTERNATIONAL DEFICITS

Have you ever sensed while traveling abroad that Americans are both loved and hated just a little more than other foreigners? It might be understandable why people may have problems with the American attitude—we can be pretty confident, direct, and headstrong. But why are we favored at the same time? It ain't our personalities. It's what we carry in our wallets—the good old American greenback.

America has been a world leader since World War II—in fact, we've been *the* world leader. We are the greatest military power, we have the biggest market, and we hold exaggerated influence in international councils. (There I go, talking like the kind of American the world loves to hate!) For sixty-five years it has been easy to identify the keystone of our global economic might: the U.S. dollar. The strength of our democracy and the dominance of our economy have made the dollar a powerful tool of global commerce. In fact, the rest of the world has long used the dollar as the international currency of choice. American money has become the world's money. But recent economic troubles have caused a lot of foreign investors to take another look at the dollar. That's why I worry that our fiscal crisis is damaging not only our lifestyle at home, but our standing in the world.

We have become as addicted to deficits and debt in our international policy as we have at home. We now import much more than we export, a practice that leaves us with a sizable trade deficit— that is, the difference between what we buy and sell internationally. In recent years we have spent hundreds of billions, and in 2008 over 700 billion, more dollars in the global economy than we have taken in. During my lifetime, we have also gone from being the world's largest creditor nation to the world's largest debtor nation internationally. These trends already have left us more vulnerable to international rivals. Unless we clean up our act, we will pass on a much more dangerous world to our heirs.

We have largely inflicted these troubles on ourselves. You know my bottom line on that practice. It is fiscally irresponsible and morally reprehensible, and it threatens our collective future. This chapter examines how that profligacy is hurting America's international standing and looks at how we can avoid an even bigger crisis down the road.

I can offer you my own perspective on these issues. Though I mainly served the U.S. government, as comptroller general from 1998 to 2008, I also served on the board of the International Organization of Supreme Audit Institutions, the U.N.-affiliated professional organization for the top national audit institutions in 189 countries around the world, and as chairman of the first ever Strategic Planning Task Force for that organization. Today, I still watch international finance closely as chairman of the Independent Audit Advisory Committee of the United Nations, and I was recently named as one of fewer than four hundred global members of the Trilateral Commission. These and other positions have put me in touch with government and economic leaders around the world, and some of their private doubts about U.S. strength and steadfastness should set off alarm bells in Washington.

FINANCING AN ISOLATED NATION

I tell my interlocutors abroad that if you want to understand the United States, don't look just at our policies today, look at our history and culture. We began our nationhood determined to set ourselves apart from the currents of international affairs, even if that looked to our foreign partners and rivals like a world-be-damned policy. You can still see strong reflections of that attitude today, most recently in the policies of President Bush 43, who in many cases regarded international cooperation and compromise as a weakness.

The truth is that in our early days we saw little need for international diplomacy. The United States was a largely self-sufficient agrarian nation that exported cotton, tobacco, and other agricultural products, and imported little more than a few manufactured and luxury items. Until the federal income tax came along in 1913, we financed our national government mostly on proceeds from import duties and tariffs.

We avoided excessive debt throughout that era. Let's take special note of the year 1834. America actually got its financial act together that year and became almost debt-free. Dig out that old balance sheet, because we'll never see that condition again.

During the Civil War, trade issues played a role that is not discussed very much. England was more industrialized than the United States, but it had grown dependent on cotton, tobacco, and other agricultural exports from the southern states to supply its textile industries and to meet English consumer demand. As a result, England provided unofficial support to the Confederacy, much of which was coordinated from Bermuda, although it never officially recognized the Confederate States of America as an independent nation.

The United States finally took notice of the outside world under President Theodore Roosevelt, who is one of my favorite presidents. Among other things, TR was an internationalist who was committed to bringing the United States out of its shell and putting it on the world stage. His deployment of "the Great White Fleet" showed off America's military might.

Our power and the strength of our export economy grew with industrialization. This growth continued through two world wars and the Great Depression of the twentieth century. At the end of World War II, the United States emerged as the only major country whose mainland had escaped attack. That strength and our ingenuity and productivity catapulted us into global economic and political supremacy whether or not we wanted that status. After World War II ended, the United States alone represented more than 50 percent of the global economy. In many ways, we *were* the global economy, and the dollar was deemed to be as good as gold. In fact, the dollar was backed by gold at a fixed rate of $35 an ounce.

The trade agreements after World War II made it official: The dollar was singled out as the official currency for international commerce. We have been taking that for granted ever since. We shouldn't.

PRELUDE TO A MELTDOWN

Why does the era of the Almighty Dollar seem to be coming to a close? Without question, our success in reviving the global economy created other power centers—including Japan and Germany—that claimed their own place in the sun. The real troubles for the dollar began in 1971, when President Nixon took it off the gold standard; he acted in part because Vietnam War spending had led to inflation and deficits, prompting France and other countries to start demanding gold for their dollars. The so-called Nixon Shock sent oil prices, which were denominated in dollars, much higher. Interest rates also rose sharply.

The dollar has been less stable ever since. Now that it is no longer tethered to gold, its value has gone up or down like any other market commodity. When the value of the dollar is low, and may be headed lower, investors tend to demand higher interest rates to buy our bonds. That increases our costs, raises the size of our national debt, and gives our government less money to spend at home.

While the value of the dollar is important, the rate at which it changes value is also important. A sudden and dramatic decline in the dollar can cause serious damage to our economy.

Since our borrowing is more and more dependent on foreign lenders, our economy is becoming steadily more vulnerable to foreign influence. While total debt reached a record 122 percent of our gross domestic product (GDP) after World War II, it was all owed to Americans. Today, over 50 percent of our public debt is held by foreign lenders. And that percentage is increasing.

Why do we borrow so much money? Because we spend too much! You know from previous chapters that we Americans have become a nation of spenders, not savers. Here's how that affects our position in the world. Consider all the money, goods, and services that constantly flow into and out of the United States. The difference between what we buy and what we sell is called our trade balance. If we buy more than we sell, we have a trade deficit. We have run such a deficit for many years now. Why is that bad? Stay with me.

From a broader perspective, the trade balance combined with a few other international transactions—including dividends on investments and other transfer payments from abroad—give us what we call our current account balance. This is something like a national checking account for international transactions. Unfortunately, just like the federal government's domestic account, that checkbook is badly out of balance. In 2006, the current account deficit exceeded 6 percent of our GDP (the market value of all the goods and services we produce in a year—a little over $14 trillion in 2008). (See figure 10.) That's a very unhealthy level. It pushes down the value of the dollar and it can't be sustained over time.

When we spend money we don't have, we must borrow money to pay our bills. During the recent boom years, there were plenty of lenders out there. For years, China and other countries financed our deficit by buying our Treasury bonds at extremely low interest rates.

That was for their own good in the short term, because their bond purchases kept U.S. consumer interest rates low and housing prices high—so that America could continue to buy China's and other countries' exports. And we Americans were delighted to cooperate so we could have what we wanted no matter whether we needed it or not.

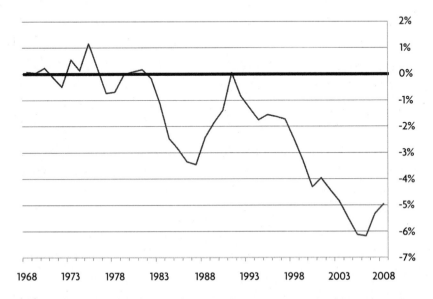

Figure 10 U.S. current account surplus and deficit as a percentage of GDP. Our international checkbook is far from balanced.

We wanted a lot. Historically, consumer spending has accounted for 60 to 65 percent of our national economic activity. But as the economy heated up, Americans went on a shopping spree, and consumer spending increased to 72 percent. This is also unhealthy and unsustainable.

Credit became cheap and easy to get. Billions of dollars in that easy money poured into the housing market, where mortgages went on sale for bargain rates, and the housing-price bubble expanded until the big pop of 2007–08 brought our entire financial system to its knees. What is the lesson? You can't spend more money than you make forever without the risk of suffering a major trauma—call it a financial heart attack.

So here's the dynamic that led to our crisis: Foreign investors flooded us with cheap money, stoking our consumer frenzy. They gave us "more than enough rope to hang ourselves," as C. Fred Bergsten, director of the Peterson Institute of International Economics, puts it. But in the end, foreigners were not to blame for what happened. We did the irresponsible spending.

THE DOLLAR'S TRAJECTORY

In the past, the preeminence of the dollar has protected us from our own worst habits. To put it bluntly, we could routinely get away with profligate spending and imprudent fiscal practices. The markets couldn't punish our currency too much because it was *the* currency.

Now that advantage is no longer quite such a sure thing. The dollar isn't nearly as strong as it was after World War II. The United States now represents about 23 percent of the global economy in 2008, down from over 50 percent after World War II—still the largest on the planet, but not utterly dominating. The dollar is on a similar downward trajectory.

The dollar has a competitor now—the euro—and a few other currencies, including the British pound and the Japanese yen, are also used in international trade. As of this writing, sixteen of the twenty-seven members of the European Union had adopted the euro as their official national currency. The United Kingdom and Denmark (who are in the European Union) and Norway and Switzerland (who are not) were the only major exceptions in western Europe.

Could the euro or another currency replace the dollar as the world's premier reserve currency? The answer is yes. In September 2007, Alan Greenspan said that it is "absolutely conceivable that the Euro will replace the dollar as reserve currency or [that it] will be traded as an equally important reserve currency." More recently, World Bank president Robert Zoellick, the former U.S. trade representative, noted that the euro provides a "respectable alternative" to the dollar and that the Chinese renminbi is likely to grow in importance. If that is true, we will have even more trouble managing our domestic and international deficits.

National treasuries around the world already are relying less on the U.S. dollar than they once did. A very important one, China, has been aggressively spending down its dollar reserves on commodities in order to hedge against a decline in the dollar's value and the potential of inflation.

I have been involved in a number of high-level meetings on these topics, and they continue into the present. In 2007, Chinese premier Wen Jiabao asked to meet with me during one of my visits with my Chinese counterpart, Li Jinhua, head of the Chinese National Audit Office. Premier Wen asked me about the projected financial condition of the U.S. government. I didn't say anything to him privately that I had not said in the United States publicly. Needless to say, the numbers spoke for themselves, and he got the message.

In early 2009, Wen stated his concern publicly. Soon after he made his statement, a leading official of China's central bank raised the question whether the world had grown too dependent on the U.S. dollar and suggested that it might explore other global currency options.

President Obama and various high-ranking U.S. economic officials tried to reassure China and others that the dollar remains as strong as ever, and that it will survive today's crisis with its power intact. Treasury Secretary Timothy Geithner traveled to China and assured a big audience at Beijing University that their country's U.S. investments were safe—but it didn't help when the assembled students greeted his comment with laughter.

The Chinese are not the only investors concerned about the fiscal behavior of the U.S. government and America's low savings rates. I have heard top officials from the Organization of Petroleum Exporting Countries (OPEC) express their own concerns on these issues. In my view, it is not a matter of if but when OPEC nations no longer use the dollar as the sole means to price oil. Kuwait, a strong ally of the United States and a key OPEC member, has already pegged its dinar to a basket of currencies to value its oil exports. This slightly reduces the attractiveness of the dollar and, more important, sends a signal to others.

THE NEXT CRISIS

China, Japan, Germany, and other countries profited greatly from America's consumption binge in recent years. But they and every other major economy on Earth were swept into the 2009 crisis to one degree or another. Most were in recession, and others, like China, grew at much slower rates.

The great engine of growth, the United States, had stopped buying nearly as much from overseas. That, plus a drop in oil prices, narrowed our current account deficit somewhat, at least for the short term. But that was good news only for us. The decline of our market forced exporters like China to look inward. If they wanted growth, they would have to expand their domestic markets. What if they failed? That would further weigh down the global economy. The financial disaster that began in the United States might be extended and deepened.

The drop in international trade probably won't help the dollar. Even under President Obama's rosiest scenario, the U.S. current account deficit will be high, putting greater pressure on the world's reserve currency before the economy recovers. After the government launched its expensive rescue and stimulus plans in late 2008, the CBO estimated that our fiscal 2009 deficit would reach an astounding 8.3 percent of GDP—more than three times the average 2.3 percent. (The OMB announced in October 2009 that the deficit for fiscal 2009 was $1.42 trillion, or 9.9 percent of GDP.) Even the 8.3 percent figure prompted concern among a number of international leaders. Obama's suggestion that they follow the United States in passing a huge domestic stimulus program was poorly received in many quarters. Czech prime minister Mirek Topolánek, whose country held the EU presidency, denounced Obama's plan as "the way to hell."

As our deficits grow in the United States, our debt to the rest of the world—which we imprudently rely on to finance our domestic shortfall—also grows. Remember, the unified budget deficit was about 1.2 percent of GDP in fiscal 2007, and 3.2 percent in fiscal 2008. As noted above, it was about 9.9 percent in fiscal 2009. If we could bring it down to about 2 percent and keep it there, that would limit our debt to the rest of the world and our current account deficit could be stabilized at 4.5 percent for the first quarter of this century—which is still too high, but not potentially catastrophic.

If we don't wake up, the next crisis could be much worse. What if we went into it with even greater budget and current account deficits? We would likely use the same strategies we used this time—loans and guarantees to ailing financial firms, interest rate cuts, and massive spending to stimulate a recovery. These measures worked this time because the world still trusts in the strength of the dollar and the safety of U.S. bonds. But what if trust in the United States erodes, either before or during the next crisis? In that dismal event, our economy would face skyrocketing interest rates at best, and at worst a flight from the dollar to the euro or the yen.

If that happens, farewell to America as the world's economic powerhouse. It's not inevitable, but it's not inconceivable either. The dollar is weaker now than it was before the crisis. Washington's stimulus program—which essentially involves spending money we don't have—risks lowering the dollar's value and stoking inflation. The Federal Reserve, which manages our money supply, has thrown all of its powers into reviving the markets by lowering interest rates to almost nothing; specifically, it reduced the Fed discount rate to .25 percent, a dramatic reduction from past levels. It also extended easy credit to bail out our financial industry—again at the risk of weakening the dollar.

It's worth understanding what the Fed is up to. In normal times, it has a conservative balance sheet of assets (mostly U.S. Treasury bonds) and liabilities (mostly the U.S. paper currency in circulation). During the market crisis, however, the Fed's balance sheet has more than doubled, from $870 billion to more than $2 trillion. Why has it grown? In addition to buying U.S. government bonds, the Fed has extended various kinds of credits to the American finance industry as a way of reviving our financial markets. The Fed really was the lender of last resort to these ailing firms, and it insists the loans are safe. But, well, would you have loaned money to the U.S. finance industry at that point? And some of these investments make even the Fed governors blanch. Our chief monetary authority has billions invested to keep the AIG insurance company on life support and to back J. P. Morgan Chase's purchase of the failed Bear Stearns investment company. How does the Fed finance all of this credit? It prints more money. Any way you look at it, the Fed's bloated balance sheet is not as conservative as it used to be.

We shouldn't worry too much right now. Our financial system appears to have weathered the crisis of 2007–08. But America's standing as the model for global capitalism has been damaged. Don't underestimate the extent to which such psychological factors will weaken our leadership in the next global financial crisis. Right now we have a mortgage-related subprime crisis. Let me emphasize that we need to avoid a supersubprime crisis—one that could result from a loss of international confidence in the ability of the United States to put its own financial house in order. That kind of crisis would lead not to another recession, but to an outright global depression.

Is this a real possibility? You better believe it is, given how weak the global financial system is right now. The big agencies that judge the creditworthiness of corporations have been taking a close look lately at the financial foundations of sovereign nations. The United States has long had a Triple-A bond rating, classifying it as the safest possible investment (a status that helps countries, like companies, sell their bonds for lower interest rates). When in early 2009 I wrote an op-ed for the *Financial Times* expressing concern that the Triple-A rating of the United States may be at risk, domestically many people tended to discount such a possibility, but not internationally. After all, creditworthiness should not be just about the risk of the default. It should also be about the value of the currency used to repay the loan. In the op-ed I said that the outcome depends on how Washington resolves the health care reform debate and whether it will take other concrete actions to put the nation's financial house in order.

But in May 2009, within ten days of my op-ed being published, we received an indirect warning. That's when Standard & Poor's, one of the premier bond-rating agencies, changed its outlook for the United Kingdom's Triple-A rating from "stable" to "negative."

This action meant that, while the rating had not been downgraded immediately, the likelihood that it would be had increased significantly. That action was widely seen as a shot across Britain's bow and a possible precursor to a downgrade of Britain's debt.

What many people overlooked was how Britain's fiscal record compared with ours. The answer? A mixed picture, but certainly there are real areas of concern. Our budget deficit, total federal debt, and foreign debt as a percentage of the economy were as bad as or worse than Britain's. They had some fiscal health problems at home; for example, Britain's tax rates were already high, giving it less room to raise more tax revenue. But some of its fiscal policies were better than ours. Britain does not write a blank check for its health care costs and has already begun to reform its equivalent of our Social Security system.

That's not to say that the United Kingdom's or the United States' credit ratings will definitely be downgraded soon. However, both likely will be at some point unless definitive actions are taken. We do have a history of getting our act together before we hit a wall. Hopefully that will be the case again, because the world is becoming a much more competitive place.

The rest of the world is busy drawing lessons from the recent financial collapse. The U.S. market crash taught many countries in the developing world that they need to hoard hard-currency reserves—and the dollar is still the strongest. Those healthy reserves, they hope, will give them insurance to ride out the next financial crisis.

How do they accumulate dollars? Well, they can do what China did starting in the 1990s: keep the value of their own currencies low so that they can export low-cost goods to the United States in exchange for dollars. China accumulated $2 trillion in reserves by the time the crisis hit. Now India may have plans to amass reserves of $1 trillion, according to experts monitoring its policy. And many others will choose the same path. If this scenario plays out, once again the U.S. dollar will be overvalued compared to other world currencies, once again the United States will face an oversized current account deficit, and once again we could have an overheated economy heading for meltdown.

HOW TO AVOID THE BIG ONE

How do we keep history from repeating itself, with even more disastrous consequences? Our work starts at home. After we recover from our recession, we have to take the steps I'm outlining in this book to restore our fiscal health. Once growth returns, we need to get control of federal spending to ensure that our recent free-spending and loose money policies do not usher in a devastating round of inflation.

Simply speaking, we have to balance our domestic and international checkbooks—or at least come close by cutting our current account deficit to roughly 3 percent of GDP, half its level before our latest crisis. There are several possible ways to do that. We could force our economy to run at a consistently slow rate of growth so that we spend less money on foreign imports, a strategy that no American leader ever would adopt. Or we could entice and cajole Americans into saving more of their money so that we keep more dollars at home, a strategy that might work temporarily but probably will not become a permanent feature of American life (though I'm trying!). We could also work harder to enforce equitable trade. The global trading rules we put into effect after World War II are not strong enough for a shrinking, borderless world. We need tougher rules to prevent unfair currency manipulation, to regulate multinational corporations that answer to no government, and to stop protectionism.

Free trade makes sense for America. If we try to protect our auto industry, steel industry, and the like from foreign competition, they will go downhill faster than they already have. But that doesn't mean that our trading partners should have unfettered access to our markets while they keep us out of theirs, or while they condone exploitative labor practices and do too little to protect the environment. In the end, if we want to maintain our leadership abroad, we need free trade and fair trade to serve a healthy economy at home.

We have to choose our battles carefully. We can't compete on wages with most of the world, and frankly we don't want to. That would hurt our own standard of living. Instead, we have to enhance the American talents for innovation, productivity, quality, and reliability. Our researchers have guided the world into the age of information technology, and we have to stay ahead of that curve. In the global production chain, America must remain the nation that comes up with the new ideas and puts them to use for everybody's benefit. Our wages will be higher, but the value we add to a new technology and our superior productivity will keep us ahead in the global market. Let's lead the way in the next round of information technology and telecommunications, alternative energy sources (so-called green jobs), and biotechnology.

How do we create an economy smart enough to fill that role? Getting our health care and social spending under control and restoring fiscal sanity are necessary steps. That will help us play up our other advantages: our political stability, our rule of law, and the sheer size—and voraciousness—of the American market. But we also have to smarten up our workforce. America doesn't rank among the top twenty nations in the world in high-school-level math and science proficiency. Our high school system does a poor job of teaching civic responsibility and personal financial literacy as well. About one in three high school students fails to graduate, according to the America's Promise Alliance, a proeducation partnership—a record that we simply must improve if we are to employ young people coming out of our educational system in the tech-intensive jobs of our future.

Our postsecondary educational system has long had ascendancy, but it is very expensive and becoming more so. America's universities are the best in the world—factories of ideas and experimentation. Now we have to work to keep them that way. The hallmark of their success has been their openness to the best and the brightest students from around the world. But after 9/11, we tightened our visa requirements and began turning away talented scholars applying to study and do research in the United States. It took until 2007 for the State Department to resume issuing as many standard student visas as it awarded in 2001.

We lost a lot of brilliant prospects in those six years, and they have now learned there are options other than U.S. schools for pursuing their educational goals. These options will only increase in the future with advances in Internet learning and the establishment of strategic partnerships among leading universities in the United States and around the world. At a time when other university systems are boosting their resources and trying to copy the American model, we have to make sure that we maintain our own standards of robust, open, innovative higher education.

Education is the top priority for building our future, but there are others. We need to help small businesses capitalize on their export opportunities. After all, small businesses represent the engines of growth and innovation in our economy. They also employ the most people. The federal government needs to help them in the same way that Japan and other nations have helped their domestic businesses export more.

Finally, there is the issue I'll spend most of the rest of this book analyzing: We must use this moment to shape up and smarten up our government. It was the failure of government to see the economic warning signs and take corrective action that got us into this mess. I'll tell you from my inside perspective how we can fashion a more strategic, future-focused, results-oriented, leaner, more efficient, more responsive, and more representative government in

Washington. Take hope, fellow Americans. We can build a better future if we are prepared to start work on an agenda of transformational reforms. Let's begin by taking a look at the basic changes we need in one of the core functions of the federal government: national defense.

Nine

GETTING CONTROL
OF THE PENTAGON

As you know by now, Social Security, Medicare, Medicaid, and other "mandatory" programs (those whose spending is on autopilot) took up over 60 percent of our federal budget in fiscal 2008. The rest of the budget spending is discretionary—that is, the president and Congress can divide it up as they see fit. About half of that money—or approximately 20 percent of the entire federal budget—goes for defense. While it's been higher as a percentage at other times (it was 46 percent of the federal budget in 1968), it still represents a major part of our budget and one in which hard choices are not always being made.

I remember coming into office in 1998 and feeling the need to get much closer to defense issues in general, and the Pentagon's way of doing business in particular. I took a number of steps to do so over the years. Based on that experience, I came to the conclusion that we have built the best fighting forces in the world at a very high cost and with a huge amount of waste. And the nation's defense strategy is not as comprehensive, integrated, and future-focused as it needs to be.

The Obama administration proposed a $775 billion defense budget for fiscal 2010, including funding for Iraq, Afghanistan, and other overseas military operations. By some estimates, that's more than the rest of the world—combined—spends for national defense. There is some dispute here, since there are lots of ways to categorize defense spending, and not all countries are as transparent about their military expenditures as we are. It is safe to say, however, that of all the nations in the world the United States spends by far the most money on defense.

No responsible person would argue that we should weaken our military effectiveness. We need a strong, smart, and adaptable military force as a vital tool in the war on terror. Building a cutting-edge, high-tech fighting machine costs billions each year in research and development alone. We also have to pay the highly trained professional servicemen and -women who defend our soil. And so my point is not that our nation can be protected on the cheap. Rather, we have to clean up the waste in the system, which is contributing significantly to our fiscal crisis.

No elected official wants to appear weak on defense or anything less than supportive of our troops. And no congressman wants to go back to his district and tell people that he has voted against a weapon that provides them with jobs. For these and other reasons, some of them psychological, it's simply hard for Congress to say no to the Pentagon. Nonetheless, if we are going to regain our fiscal sanity, we have to start asking tougher questions about our Pentagon budget. Have we built our military machine as cost-effectively as we should have? And have we retooled our fighting forces adequately for the challenges of today and tomorrow? I think you can guess my answers to those questions.

DEMANDS OF THE TWENTY-FIRST CENTURY

In order to count itself as a well-run organization during a time of fiscal crisis, the Pentagon—like the rest of government—must focus on the future and on achieving real results while also ensuring that it is giving us the best value for our money. In military terms, we need a forward-leaning, risk-based, and objectives-focused strategy.

This involves more than looking at the history of shooting wars or Cold War standoffs. Our military planners have the much tougher job of anticipating our needs in an age of terror and nuclear proliferation, and building a military apparatus to meet those challenges given the resources we have available.

Are we well enough prepared to handle weapons of mass destruction—suitcase nukes, biological agents, chemical weapons? What's our best defense against cyber-warfare and terrorist cells that organize without regard to nationalities or borders? How do we best respond to the little wars that can turn into big wars, or to the civil strife that can create breeding grounds for terrorists in the developing world? And how can we be sure that global commerce keeps flowing and our national interests are protected even if we don't have to fire a shot? After all, as Teddy Roosevelt said, the best policy is to "speak softly and carry a big stick." He was right, but the size of the stick should bear some proportionality to real and likely risks.

Above all, we face the challenge of international terrorism. This is not an entirely new phenomenon. Thomas Jefferson had to contend with the Barbary pirates who terrorized commercial ships of the world powers in the early 1800s. The pirates, hiding along the shores of Tripoli and other ports in North Africa, were much better organized and better armed than today's Somali pirates. In many ways, they were a sea-based force akin to al-Qaeda. But today's terrorists, of course, are much more lethal and mobile. They have no permanent base or strong organization. To respond to their threat, we must find new ways of conceiving and executing our military operations—rising above our own bureaucratic restraints.

Terrorism in particular is a crucial area in which we need to change how we think about risk. The Pentagon must maximize value and manage risk in light of our current and expected resources. Note that I say we should *manage* risk, not minimize it. Why? Because in reforming government (as in many other endeavors), we can't maximize value if we are concerned only with minimizing risk. Especially during a time of increasingly constrained resources, we have to determine an acceptable degree of risk and draw the line at spending excessively in a vain effort to eliminate risk altogether.

A more fiscally prudent defense strategy will, in the end, involve carefully identifying the most dangerous threats that face us and allocating resources to meet those threats accordingly. So let's rethink our defense strategy and handle the risks as need be. Our first principle may be that the era of massive military force is over. Our job in government today is to improve our economy and our administrative efficiency and effectiveness without compromising national security. This means maintaining an effective deterrent and the option of lethal force in a way that is both affordable and sustainable.

Don't get me wrong; I am not playing down the importance of military power or slighting the successes of our fighting forces in the Persian Gulf, Iraq, Afghanistan, or anywhere else. Nor am I suggesting that we hand off essential military work to civilians. Under the Pentagon's "total force" concept, it has begun using more civilian contractors to supplement its military personnel. We all have read about the abuses by contractors working as security guards and interrogators in Iraq, and about the questionable contracts that were awarded without competitive bids. Congress needs to consider which jobs are "inherently governmental" and avoid using contractors to do work that should be done by the military or civil servants.

America's military training, technology, and logistics capabilities are second to none. But our success is often coupled with billions of dollars of waste—and our planning process emphasizes dividing up the pie of available resources rather than strategically assessing real threats and corresponding needs.

COMBATING WASTE

What do I mean by "waste"? It's one of those slippery words I've been pointing out that doesn't mean the same thing in Washington as it does in Webster's dictionary. In Washington, "waste" too often means "programs other than mine." After years on the front lines in Washington, I've also found that one person's "waste" is another's "investment."

We need a better definition—something that a professional accountant and auditor like me can consider objectively. Here's the one I used when I oversaw the federal government's budget: Waste is the failure to give taxpayers as a whole reasonable value for their money because of an inappropriate act or omission by a party with discretionary control over government assets or resources.

Sorry, that's a bit of a mouthful, but I chose all of these words carefully and for good reason. This definition covers everybody who can dip into the public coffers for personal, bureaucratic, or special interests rather than staying focused on our nation's collective best interests. It covers the members of Congress who want to develop a weapons system to create jobs in their districts—not because we need the system. It covers the powerful contractor who lobbies Congress to adopt a technology that he has mastered—again, whether or not we actually need it. It covers military officers who want to buy their dreams with our money, elected officials who try to secure contributions and votes with our money, political appointees who push an ideological agenda with our money, and civil servants who negotiate bloated contracts with our money. It covers the government, which pays performance bonuses to contractors who are late and over budget and who fail to meet performance expectations. After all, it's easy to spend someone else's money. Washington does it all the time.

The truth is that all too frequently what drives the Pentagon budget is not our security needs for the future but the wants of today. The word used in the Pentagon is "requirements." I put that word in quotation marks because "requirements" is another of those words with a special Washington meaning. In the Pentagon, "requirements" might be no more than the wish lists produced by the various service branches. Creating the budget is largely a bottom-up process, in which the branches put together lists of hardware, personnel, bases, and other proposals that are all aggregated—often with only a modest review by the White House—and sent to Congress for action. And believe it or not, when determining what our requirements are, by law, the Pentagon is not supposed to consider how much they will cost. No wonder our military has a spending problem!

Yes, of course planning is part of the process, but it's not done in any properly designated and coordinated way. Like other bureaucracies, the Army, Navy, Air Force, and Marine Corps fight to hold their turf in the budget contest. And within their own establishments, there is huge pressure to preserve what they have—including expensive weapons systems that we might not need at all or excessive quantities of things we do need.

On the other side of the coin, nobody in the civilian world who is prospering from the Pentagon's generous spending wants to stop milking all those cash cows. Watch what happens when the Pentagon tries to cut a weapons program that benefits a powerful corporation—or when it proposes closing an outmoded military base that benefits the constituents of various congressmen and senators. Let's call it like it is: Too many decisions in Washington are made based on local economic considerations rather than our national interest.

When this planning process, politically tainted as it is, leads to the approval of a new weapons system—anything from a rifle to a jet engine to a supersonic fighter—the spending really starts in the production process, in the form of rising costs, broken deadlines, and changing specifications. We tried to keep track of these costs at the Government Accountability Office. One tool was the "high risk list" that we maintained to identify federal programs and functions that were subject to greater risk of fraud, waste, abuse, or mismanagement, or simply of failing to achieve their objectives. GAO's 2009 High Risk Report contained thirty high risk items, of which fifteen related directly or indirectly to the Defense Department, and fourteen of the thirty required congressional action to effectively address. GAO supplemented this list with a periodic "quick look report" on major Pentagon weapons systems.

A few eagle-eyes in Congress helped immeasurably. In the Senate, John McCain, a decorated Vietnam War veteran and former prisoner of war, generally led the charge against waste in the Defense Department. By his reckoning early in 2009, based on statistics from GAO's audit and evaluation work, the cost of ninety-five major weapons systems had grown by 30 percent during development, rising to a total of about $1.3 trillion.

The Pentagon, of course, has the main responsibility for managing and overseeing these projects. But no matter who is in charge, the system is so fundamentally flawed that billions of dollars in waste is virtually guaranteed every year. It's pretty clear that the biggest area of Pentagon waste involves acquisitions and contracting. (In fact, that's a major high-risk area throughout the government.) By the time I left the GAO, we had identified fifteen systemic problems with the Pentagon's procurement systems, many of which were shared by other federal agencies. I call these the "fundamental fifteen." Among other shortcomings, we highlighted bad planning, bloated contracts, congressional meddling, and the "plug and pray" approach to complex projects, in which the Pentagon divides the available funds for a program by the current cost per unit and prays that Congress will allocate additional funds to acquire more units. And procurement was only one problem. As of 2009, the Defense Department occupied nine of twenty-six high-risk areas on the GAO's government-wide list. Many of these warnings had been on the list since its creation in 1992.

There are lots of incentives to grab a piece of the budget bounty in the Pentagon, and very few to manage your share efficiently. I saw this myself during the approximately eight years I served as an ex officio and nonvoting member of the Defense Business Board (DBB). The DBB, created during Secretary Donald Rumsfeld's tenure, comprises top-level civilians and former senior flag officers (three- and four-star generals and admirals), and it made a number of solid recommendations designed to improve the Defense Department's business practices. The DBB came up with ideas to improve military health care, mail delivery, and recruiting, among other things. But after a while, it became clear that many organizations and individuals within the Pentagon's five walls had an effective pocket veto over any meaningful changes to the status quo.

They got that power because in the Pentagon, any significant decision has to make its way through innumerable in-boxes. For example, when I participated in CAPSTONE, a training program for generals and admirals, I was told that more than twenty different units had to approve the activation of as few as twenty National Guard or Reserve members before the proposed deployment was sent to the secretary of defense, who had to give final approval. That kind of process is one factor behind my belief that if the Pentagon bureaucracy were 25 percent smaller, it might be 50 percent more effective.

What's really amazing is that nobody is in charge of shaping up the Pentagon's business practices. The Defense Department does have a position for a deputy chief management officer, approved by law in 2007. But in Washington's most rank-conscious bureaucracy, the new position ranks so low that it is unlikely to have any real effectiveness. As of this writing, the job is still open and has never been filled.

What the Pentagon needs instead is a position equivalent in rank to the deputy secretary—level two in the hierarchy—with at least a five-year appointment to carry it beyond the term of any single administration. That would help attract a highly qualified professional with a proven record of transformational success. The new chief operating officer (COO) or chief management officer (CMO) would be in a position to transform the way the Pentagon does business. The COO or CMO should have a performance-based contract to help ensure that the new officer does just that. Don't hold your breath waiting for the Defense Department to agree to that dose of responsibility. After all, everyone is for accountability until they are the ones being held accountable.

COMING TO TERMS WITH THE MESS

If and when such a new COO or CMO signs on, good luck to the person who gets the job; he or she will need it. The Pentagon's business operations are a mess. This huge bureaucracy is the only major agency whose books are so jumbled that it cannot withstand a financial audit. While officials had planned to have their books in shape and audited by the time the Bush 43 administration came to office, the Defense Department is not expected to be able to go through such an audit for another ten years. Where do you start when the Pentagon has thousands of information systems that cannot even communicate with each other?

After September 11, 2001, the Defense Department's accounting books became more complicated, not less so. As I told you in an earlier chapter, that's when the Bush administration started financing the so-called global war on terror with "supplemental" appropriations, a strategy that hid the cost of the war in the regular defense budget.

The "emergency" and "supplemental" appropriations for Afghanistan and Iraq were not subject to the normal budget process and received even less scrutiny and accountability than the regular Pentagon budget. They were simply charged to our national credit card. Who knows exactly what we bought with those multiple billions? I don't and the Pentagon doesn't.

President Obama, to his credit, proposed to include the costs of Afghanistan and Iraq in the regular Pentagon budget starting in fiscal 2010. He did this acknowledging the reality that some related costs would continue for a number of years. That's a more honest approach, and it improves transparency. However, it also increases the federal government's and the Pentagon's baseline budget without any guarantee that we will be able to account for all the money. Remember President Reagan's call to "trust but verify."

Since Obama's truth-telling strategy makes the Pentagon's budget base much larger, Congress and the administration will need to work hard to be sure that all nonrecurring costs attributable to Iraq, Afghanistan, and other military and support operations are eliminated when we draw down our forces. As is the case with almost any department or program in Washington, it's easy to add numbers to a budget, but very difficult to subtract them.

THE PSYCHOLOGY OF "WAR"

Despite all its management problems, the Pentagon has huge and unparalleled influence on Capitol Hill. When a general or admiral in gleaming uniform, sitting ramrod straight, puts a list of "requirements" before a congressional committee, it's very hard for members of Congress to say no. We are talking about national defense, after all. How do you turn down a warrior demanding, say, a new fighter or ship, when the lack of it could lead to American deaths? How do you turn down a request for more benefits to support our servicemen and -women whose job is to put their lives on the line for America?

There is a psychological dimension in the give-and-take between Washington's civilian and military leaders that is not often acknowledged. A lot of it has to do with the way our definition of "war" has changed over the years. In the dictionary, it's defined as "open and armed conflict between nations." This makes sense to me and is generally consistent with how our nation defined it for more than 150 years. That takes us to the last war we actually declared, World War II. We have been through a number of serious national conflicts since then—in Korea, Vietnam, the Persian Gulf, Afghanistan, and Iraq. But in none of those conflicts was the constitutional mandate fulfilled that war must be declared by Congress.

I don't know about you, but I am concerned that our nation has lost sight of what war is. "It is a good thing that war is so terrible," General Robert E. Lee said, "or we would come to love it." War is too terrible to take lightly. It demands of us a commitment of American lives and treasure for the benefit our country. For that reason, as I said in chapter 3 about principles, when we fight a war, Congress should declare it—not just pass resolutions of support. And all Americans should participate to support it in some meaningful way.

That sense of shared national defense started to erode during the conflict in Korea, which we called a "police action" and failed to declare as a war. It eroded further in Vietnam, another undeclared war, where young men of means and education found ways to avoid the draft. After President Nixon ended the draft in 1973, we built a leaner, more professional military machine that essentially has stood apart from the larger American society ever since. Like a big corporation, the military recruits its young professionals by offering a good salary, generous benefits, and the promise of personal fulfillment ("Be All You Can Be"; "An Army of One"). The great majority of Americans support our people in uniform, but without that old sense of personal involvement. When it's time to fight, we leave it to the one-half of one percent of us who are military professionals.

The two wars we are fighting as I write this—one winding down in Iraq and one gearing up in Afghanistan—already have lasted longer than World War II and have cost billions of dollars and thousands of lives. If you want my opinion, I would say that invading Afghanistan after 9/11 was justified, since the Taliban government had provided safe harbor to al-Qaeda, but the invasion of Iraq was not. I make this statement despite the fact that our son Andy served as a Marine Corps officer and was in the first wave of the invasion to liberate Iraq in 2003. Andy and the hundreds of thousands of military personnel who were part of Operation Iraqi Freedom did their job well. Fortunately, Andy came home safe and sound, but thousands of other Americans and Iraqis died and tens of thousands have been maimed or otherwise affected for life.

There was a time when soldiers and civilians were the same people fighting for the same cause. During World War II, virtually all Americans had a role in our nation's war effort. America's young people joined the ranks or were drafted. Their parents in many cases worked in the industries that built a great military machine from scratch. If you were old enough to fight, you either fought or promoted the war effort in some other way, like working in a factory that supported the war, paying higher taxes, or buying war bonds.

Today that is not true. War has become a presidential prerogative, endorsed by Congress, and sometimes after the fact. We citizens may or may not be asked to pay for it (as inconspicuously as possible), then we go about our lives essentially ignoring it. I'll leave it to others to argue whether that's a good way to run a democracy. But it sure is a terrible way to build transparency and accountability into our Defense Department.

If anything, the divide between military service people, elected officials, and Main Street Americans is growing. Since the creation of the all-volunteer force, fewer and fewer elected officials have military experience. In addition, an ever-smaller percentage of the American population has direct military experience. Simply in terms of the balance of power, this growing gap puts elected officials at a disadvantage when questioning the military and results in a divide between those who serve our country and those who benefit from that service.

Congress, of course, reflects the larger population: There's a big disconnect between civilian and military. The numbers fluctuate, but in the 111th Congress, which convened in January 2009, only 121 of our 535 senators and representatives are military veterans, and according to many news sources, fewer than a dozen have had sons or daughters serving in Iraq, as our son Andy did, or in Afghanistan. In a situation like that, where most of the people who control the purse strings have no personal stake in our military, how do they determine how much is too much in the defense budget? How do they acknowledge bad planning, excess, and waste—and say no? It's not easy.

It's time to start taking our wars seriously again—including how we pay for them. Too many people have had a free ride for too long while others have sacrificed. When we fight a war, Congress should declare it, and that declaration should be coupled with a surtax to pay for the war. If we followed this course of action, I can assure you that we would think much more seriously before committing our human and financial resources to armed conflicts.

There aren't many politicians who will advocate cutting back the defense budget during these challenging times—but I'll advocate it. The truth is, just because the money relates to defense, homeland security, or another laudable or critical area does not mean that the cost is justified. Given current and projected deficits, we must justify all of our budgets, including the defense budget. That's the only way to keep costs under control.

THE ELEMENTS OF REFORM

The stewards of taxpayer money have to develop more courage and thicker skin when they take on the Pentagon budget. When that wish list of weapons systems and personnel benefits arrives, each item has to be considered against our actual threat-based needs for today and tomorrow. Each proposal needs to be considered in light of what is affordable and sustainable over time.

Defense Secretary Robert Gates and the Obama administration have taken some initial steps to question the Pentagon's appetite for major weapons systems and are challenging several marginal programs. The Congress also enacted a defense acquisition reform bill that was passed unanimously by both the House and the Senate and signed by the president. This bill was influenced significantly by the GAO's work and, when effectively implemented, will save the taxpayers billions of dollars a year. It addresses some but not all of the "fundamental fifteen" issues noted earlier. It's a positive step, but much, much more remains to be done.

The first thing to ask—and keep asking—about a weapons system is, do we need it? The second is, how many do we need? You have heard stories of the military spending billions on outmoded weapons, but I will tell you a story with a relatively happy ending. In 1994, the Army began developing the Crusader, a rapid-fire howitzer designed to perform twice as well as the old Paladin weapon it was to replace. The Crusader might have been a valuable tool in a European ground war against the Soviet Union and its allies—but nobody seemed to notice that the Cold War had been over for nearly half a decade before we *started* work on the Crusader. Only in 2002, after 9/11 had shown us that no howitzer was going to help us win the war on terror, did Defense Secretary Rumsfeld order an end to the $11 billion Crusader program. By that time, we had already spent over $2 billion. At least we saved the balance!

The predictable opponents sprang up to oppose Rumsfeld's move. Representatives from Oklahoma, where the Crusader was to be manufactured, fought to save their cash cow. Army lobbyists warned that canceling the weapon would cost American lives. But in the end, Congress went along and terminated the Crusader—backed by the obvious and overwhelming evidence that we just didn't need the thing.

Sometimes we do need a new weapon proposed by one of the service branches. Then the question becomes, how many of them do we need? You have to keep asking that. Air Force planners conceived the F-22 Raptor fighter in the 1980s as a plane designed to maintain air superiority over the Soviets. In recent years, with the Soviet air force long out of the picture, the Pentagon expanded the mission of the Raptor to include ground attack and intelligence capabilities in an effort to keep it relevant, but the Raptor was not a very economical way to deploy these new capabilities.

Production of more than six hundred advanced fighters originally was supposed to begin in 1994, but that schedule slipped by almost a decade. All along, Congress and the Pentagon chipped away at the program without killing it. As of this writing, supporters of the Raptor program seek to increase the number of aircraft beyond the 187 already procured through 2009, further adding to the estimated $60 billion in total program cost to date. The Air Force has already taken delivery of more than a hundred of the fighters but has yet to actually deploy them in combat.

We have cut back production and plan to shut down the assembly line in 2011, but you still have to ask: Exactly how are we going to use that many planes? Why do we need more? They cost roughly $260 million each, and we could do a lot of other things with that money. After all, money spent on items that represent wants rather than true needs is money robbed from systems that actually are needed. To his credit, President Obama has proposed to cease acquiring additional F-22s. We have enough already, and we need the money that will be saved to modernize our aging tactical fighter wings with larger numbers of aircraft that cost much less per copy. One such fighter is the Joint Strike Fighter, which is being built for several military services as well as several of our allies.

In fairness, the Air Force is not the only service with mismatches between its wants and our needs. Similar questions can be raised about the Army's Future Combat Systems, the Navy's DD(X) destroyer, and the Marine Corps' V-22 helicopter, among others. Fortunately, the Obama Administration is starting to take a hard look at weapons systems in order to separate the true needs from wants.

Bloated weapons programs make up only a portion of the challenge for anyone trying to control Pentagon costs. Think of the expense of supporting a professional army, especially when it's in the field during a time of war. We have to recruit those soldiers with good salaries; generous health, pension, and other benefits; tax preferences; educational opportunities; and the promise of retirement after only twenty years of service.

When I was at the GAO, we calculated that as of 2005, the average annual cost of keeping an American serviceman or -woman in uniform was $114,000 a year. To put this in perspective, median household income at the time was less than $50,000 a year. When I told members of Congress these figures in briefings, they were shocked. Not even leaders of the Senate and House Armed Services Committees had any idea how costly our military compensation program was.

Nonetheless, Congress continued to support the costly expansion of the military, including Guard and Reserve forces, and veterans benefit programs, even though these expenditures would not have been justified by any independent analysis. This is just another example of the government spending taxpayer money without any accountability.

We must consider whether our personnel costs are sustainable. I don't believe they are. We need to engage in a comprehensive review and reassessment of how to bring them down so we can meet our national security needs in a more affordable and sustainable manner.

The cost of keeping our National Guard and Reserve troops at the ready is already high. When these weekend warriors signed up for duty, they anticipated attending drills close to home while picking up extra pay as well as attractive education, medical, and retirement benefits. In many cases, it hasn't worked out that way. Because the regular branches have downsized over the years, many Guard and Reserve units have been called up for long periods of active duty in Iraq and Afghanistan. Guardsmen and reservists have been pulled away from their families and sent into harm's way again and again, in some cases with inferior equipment and training.

We can talk about the human toll of that sacrifice, but my job here is to point out the financial cost of recruiting Guard and Reserve volunteers in these circumstances. Rather than modernizing the Guard and Reserve model, Washington has decided simply to throw more of our money at the problem. Among other benefits, those who have compiled ninety days of aggregate service after 9/11 qualify for an enhanced GI Bill that pays full in-state college tuition and fees, a monthly housing allowance, and an annual stipend for books and supplies. They are also eligible to be part of the military health system, with huge taxpayer subsidies. That's a better deal than our returning veterans from World War II, Korea, and Vietnam got in their GI Bill.

In short, our all-volunteer military may be more professional, but keeping the troops in uniform is also a lot more expensive. You won't find anybody more promilitary than I am. We couldn't be prouder of our son Andy's service and of the contribution he and his fellow warriors have made to our national security. But I still have to ask, as a patriot, whether we must do more to control the expanding personnel and other costs of our all-volunteer fighting forces. In my view, the answer is yes.

Like all armies, ours is an organization of tooth and tail. That is, our military employs warriors who fight at the front, risking their lives every moment, and it employs people in the rear who support the warriors from positions out of the line of fire. Both of these roles are important; however, it's wrong to give all of our service people equal pay and benefits just because they wear the same basic uniform. Should a combat sergeant at the front get the same basic level of pay and benefits as a supply sergeant in the homeland who is never put at any real risk? You tell me. In my view, the idea that everybody in the service deserves recruitment and retention bonuses and the same long list of benefits is bunk. Service members' pay and benefits should be based on their skills and the risks they actually incur.

By no means am I suggesting that we treat our men and women in uniform unfairly. They all have taken jobs of service to our country. But I am saying that in this time of genuine fiscal crisis, we can't throw money at our defense programs blindly. We have to stop saluting the uniform so reflexively and start requiring the Pentagon to create commonsense spending plans.

Among other things, the Pentagon must come to new terms with its contractors. My almost-ten-year tenure as comptroller general left me with the clear opinion that we have become overly reliant on contractors. In addition, we have used contractors in inappropriate roles and in some cases continue to do so. Such was clearly the case with intelligence, interrogation, and certain personnel protection services in Iraq. The time to engage in a comprehensive review of the "inherently governmental" concept has come.

Common sense dictates that the services base their strategies on a carefully determined profile of our twenty-first-century defense needs. It tells us that the Army, Navy, Air Force, and Marine Corps should integrate their budgets, putting together a common schedule of weapons and other needs along with funding priorities designed to address credible threats. The "requirements" they produce now, in other words, should be real requirements. Finally, we need somebody very high in the Pentagon hierarchy to spend every working day making sure that the Defense Department's business transformation is on time, within budget, and achieves the intended results.

This is especially true at a time when our defense system needs constant reevaluation and change. A 2008 report by the respected Project on National Security Reform notes that the United States' status as a world leader is jeopardized by more than unpredictable new threats; we also must face the fact that our national security "is increasingly misaligned with a rapidly changing global security environment." The report notes the need to move toward more simultaneous integration of military, diplomatic, intelligence, and other assets of American power.

Such a fundamental realignment will take far more than business as usual at the Department of Defense. I have tried to show in this chapter that the Pentagon is one sacred cow we should stop worshipping. Of all government organizations, it is one of the most effective in achieving its mission, while at the same time wasting a huge amount of money, with inadequate transparency and little accountability. For these reasons, the Pentagon is a great example of how badly our government machinery needs fixing. Our defense establishment needs to be transformed rather than reformed. And despite assertions to the contrary, the first person to call for that within the Pentagon was not Bush 43's first secretary of defense, Donald Rumsfeld; it was Army Chief of Staff General Eric Shinseki.

Despite its considerable size, the Pentagon is only a 20 percent slice of our national government—and the whole government needs fixing. Stay with me for the next section of the book, where I will discuss other key challenges. I will show you how we can stage a second American Revolution and refashion our government into a better planned, more efficient, more effective, and more representative tool of the people.

Ten

TRANSFORMING GOVERNMENT

At this point, you may very well be asking yourself where this parade of failings ends. Earlier, I led you through the developing disasters of our health and retirement programs, the inadequacies of our tax system, the waste in defense, the burdens of federal debt, and our nation's increased dependency on foreign lenders. Now I'm telling you we're also unprepared for a variety of other key twenty-first-century changes and challenges. Oh, and at the same time, we're suffering through the effects of a monster of a recession. Yes, we are going through some tough times. But don't despair. I didn't call this book "Comeback America" for nothing. Together, we can climb the mountain.

When I became comptroller general in 1998, it didn't take more than a week to see how the agency's culture, systems, processes, and performance metrics needed to be changed. The atmosphere of the place and the approaches taken by the very capable and dedicated GAO professionals were very telling. For example, I found out that I was the first comptroller general who did not regularly wear all white shirts and regularly take my coat off in a meeting. I was also the first one to lead a brainstorming session with a group of top GAO executives on core values and agency protocols. And I was the first one to insist on an agency-wide strategic plan with outcome-based performance metrics. Given these factors, I knew it was time to fasten seat belts and begin the transformation ride.

It is critically important to keep in mind that at the root of our problems is the functioning of our government—not the people, but the systems, processes, and cultures. Process is very important in any enterprise, and in the case of our government we must analyze its processes and change them as needed. In fact, as I have found in my more than fifteen years of front-line experience in Washington, having the right process can make the critical difference between success and failure when tough policy reforms and transformations are involved. And we can improve the processes of government in many ways.

It's been done before. In the late 1940s, after World War II, President Truman inherited a mess of an executive branch. It was swollen with the bureaucracy cobbled up by the New Deal to combat the Depression—when FDR established an alphabet soup of agencies from the AAA (Agricultural Adjustment Administration) to the WPA (Works Progress Administration). It was weighed down by the huge government-military-industrial complex that was created from almost nothing to fight and defeat the Axis powers.

With Germany, Japan, and much of the remainder of the industrialized world in ashes, the White House found itself virtually ruling the world. And yet America lacked the tools and mechanisms to lead in an efficient and effective manner.

It was one of those moments in American history when everybody agreed that something had to be done. Congress passed a law creating the Commission on Organization of the Executive Branch of the Government, and Democrat Truman found himself working with an old rival, former Republican president Herbert Hoover, who was named to chair it. The Hoover Commission went on to propose a reorganization of the federal government that would make the office of the presidency the most powerful institution in the world—and Truman pushed more than 70 percent of those changes through Congress.

Truman's reforms, many supported by the Hoover Commission, included creating the Central Intelligence Agency, the National Security Council, the Joint Chiefs of Staff, and the Council of Economic Advisors, among other institutions still in place today. The reforms got rid of old agencies and created new ones, all in an effort to create a more efficient and better coordinated national government. For example, it eliminated the WPA and the AAA. In addition, the General Services Administration (GSA), to give just one example, took over responsibility for housing, managing, and supplying government agencies. In doing so, the GSA consolidated the functions of the National Archives Establishment, the Federal Works Agency and its Public Buildings Administration, the Bureau of Federal Supply and the Office of Contract Settlement, and the War Assets Administration.

There have been plenty of governmental reform efforts since then. Just about every new administration launches one. They typically concentrate on "cutting the fat out of government," that is, trimming costs by reducing programs and personnel. Ronald Reagan's Grace Commission issued its report in 1984 and recommended precisely 2,478 cost-cutting, revenue-enhancing measures that it said would save $424 billion in three years. Some were implemented but most were not. In the 1990s, Vice President Al Gore took on the job of "reinventing government" during the Clinton administration. Once again the focus was on trimming waste, fraud, and abuse, as well as cutting the number of bureaucrats and regulations. Bush 43 had the President's Management Agenda, led by the White House's Office of Management and Budget. His approach was to rate each agency and measure its progress in achieving certain government-wide management goals—for example, linking resources to results, financial management, human capital strategies, and enhancing information technology and security. As with all self-evaluation systems, some ratings were inflated, especially toward the end of the administration.

All of these reform efforts after Truman's were ambitious in their way, but their goal, despite the names of some of these initiatives, was primarily to tune up the government machine, not to reengineer it. As you will see in this chapter, we need more than a tune-up. We need a major engine overhaul.

To win in this faster-paced, interconnected, interdependent, and increasingly competitive world, we need a government that can plan more strategically, identify challenges and opportunities more quickly, respond to them more adeptly, and focus on achieving real results. Is our government equipped to perform in a complex and rapidly changing environment? Not by a long shot.

There is a lot at stake. We have more economic opportunities than ever, if we can recognize them. We also face more diverse threats to our national security than ever, and we can't escape them. Some are external and some we've inflicted on ourselves. Arguably, the largest of these threats is our own fiscal irresponsibility.

WE NEED A PLAN

Despite the urgency of this agenda, despite our government's size, importance, and complexity, it often ignores the basic rules of Management 101. Consider something as basic as a strategic plan. Most entities of any significant size have one. A company might make shoes for middle-income Americans, for example, and plan to shift its manufacturing to Asia and expand its sales to Europe—

like a number of industries lately. It knows what it wants to do, lays out what it plans to do, and measures how well it succeeds.

By contrast, the U.S. government does not really know what it wants to do. Believe it or not, our federal government, which is the largest single entity on Earth, has never had a strategic plan, and it's been in business since 1789! This is, in part, because of the short-term nature of many critical positions and because our government is led by politicians and political appointees who typically stay in office only for two or three years. Washington takes in trillions and spends trillions more, but it does not have a comprehensive, integrated, forward-looking plan based on a set of principles and priorities and the outcomes it hopes to achieve. Nor does it have a way to measure its overall success.

If you ask people in the executive branch for the government's strategic plan, they'll probably give you a copy of the federal budget. (Use both hands when accepting it.) But the federal budget is merely a one-year tax and spending schedule. It is not a strategic plan, which, among other things, would identify key trends, challenges, and opportunities and outline a range of proposed actions along with the results that they are intended to achieve.

President Obama did the right thing when he issued a ten-year budget projection in his 2010 proposed budget rather than a five-year projection as President Bush had done. But, again, Obama's document did not give us a set of performance objectives that we could use to measure the government's success, or lack thereof. It's one thing to set aside billions to spend on health care reform, for example. It's another to tell us specifically how that spending will address our coverage gaps, control costs, reduce hospitalization and infection rates, and reverse obesity trends.

Today we have the worst of both worlds. Our spending often spins out of control, yet we have only the haziest notions of what that spending is intended to achieve and whether it has worked at all. We commit direct federal spending, provide government guarantees, grant tax preferences, and create regulations to address issues like savings, housing, health care, education, infrastructure, and poverty in the hope that all those actions will make a difference, but without any evidence showing whether they do.

The truth is, our main government tax and spending strategy involves little more than throwing mud at the wall and seeing what sticks. And we can't really even tell what sticks. Without any standards of measurement, all definitions of "success" and "failure" devolve to the political arena. If your party enacted the new housing stimulus program, then you can make a dozen claims to support its success. But your opponents, at the same time, can point out as many claims of its failure. We ordinary taxpayers who footed the bill can only hope that something good came out of the exercise—but we can't tell either. This is simply unacceptable and must change.

We can no longer afford the luxury of this perpetual governmental confusion. Planning should become an established part of our legislative process as well. When Congress passes a major spending program or tax policy, its members should clearly define what objectives they are trying to achieve. The executive branch should translate those objectives into concrete outcomes that we can measure. If we decide to give tax preferences to increase our savings rate, what impact do those preferences actually have on the level and distribution of our overall savings rate? If we assist financial institutions, how well do those institutions pay us back by providing increased credit or otherwise helping to achieve a specific social purpose?

Measuring success must be a key aspect of all major taxing and spending and of other government efforts as well. When our government spends money or gives tax breaks to support a program, we have to know how that program is doing to begin with, whether our tax dollars make things better or worse, and—this is very important—how that program's performance compares to similar programs, both domestically and internationally.

Whether you are a company or a country, you must have the right incentives, adequate transparency, and appropriate accountability to succeed. You really don't know how well you are doing unless you have three key sets of information: (1) how you are performing based on desired goals and objectives, including outcomes; (2) whether your performance is improving or not; and (3) how your performance compares with that of similar entities.

In many cases we already have the data we need to help us make good decisions. We know, for example, that our national savings rate is too low. The government has encouraged us to save by giving tax breaks to 401(k)s and IRAs, among other efforts. But as we have seen, our national savings rate continues to lag behind the rate of other major industrialized countries. This shows us that these incentives have not been working as intended and suggests that we need to explore alternatives. Perhaps, as I argued earlier in this book, we should consider putting in place a mandatory savings program as a supplement to a solvent, sustainable, and secure Social Security system.

HOW TO START PLANNING

How do we get the data we need to make good decisions about all of our government spending? It's not hopeless. We can start by using President Obama's first budget, for fiscal 2010, as a baseline—that is, as a new starting point in determining the programs we taxpayers are supporting and how much we are spending on each. In Washington you are allowed to use "baseline" as a verb, so I call this an exercise in re-baselining our government.

This is not a new concept. It's common for Washington to baseline its budget spending. It's easy to see how much we're spending on something this year compared with last year. But I'm talking about baselining what we do and the results we are achieving. The issue is what kind of results we are getting for the money we are investing. From that standard we can set clear, transparent objectives for our government spending programs and tax preferences and determine just as clearly whether our tax dollars are making a difference. If they are, great. If not, we need to fix them, consolidate them, make sure they all work together in coordination—or discontinue them.

Among other things, we might need to consider the proper role for the federal government and whether a realignment of federal and state responsibilities might be in order. For example, the federal government could be responsible for the basic and essential health care safety net, including the Medicaid program, while states could be responsible for all education and transportation funding.

We must ask basic questions about every major federal program and policy. Here's a simple list of questions, for starters.

- When did we put the program or policy in place?
- What conditions existed at the time?
- Have those conditions changed?
- Have we modified the program or policy to reflect those changes?
- What are we trying to accomplish?
- How do we measure success based on desired outcomes?
- How well are we doing compared to set goals and related trends, and compared to comparable countries?
- Is the program or policy still a priority for today and tomorrow?
- Are other government programs or policies intended to accomplish the same thing?
- Are similar programs and policies working in a coordinated and integrated manner?
- How well are we using the experience of others—state and local governments, nonprofit agencies, other nations—to replicate successes and avoid common mistakes?

- Can we afford and sustain this program or policy in its present form?

By asking questions like these, we could begin to do some real planning and enhance accountability in Washington. We could put ourselves in a position to ask more sophisticated questions. For example, given the resources available (a vital first consideration), where do we target our available spending so that our money makes the greatest difference?

To help us transform the government to answer questions like these, we need our own version of the Hoover Commission. We could call it the Baseline Review Commission or the Government Transformation Commission. Its primary task would be not to reformulate the organization chart of government but to revitalize its ability to plan and execute affordable and sustainable programs and policies in the best interests of all Americans. It would be comprised of selected nongovernment officials with proven success in transforming organizations.

If the strategy works, we could rationalize our governmental system as never before. President Obama, for example, has noted that he wants to make health care his top priority. In the system I'm suggesting, he would not simply set aside money in the budget for reforms. He would baseline our national health care performance according to a range of key metrics on coverage, cost, quality, personal responsibility, and other factors. He would set concrete objectives for health care and target taxpayer money and government actions to meet them. We Americans could then all see how well any reforms that are enacted into law are working and compare America's results with those of other industrialized nations.

At the same time, by putting health care at the top of our list, we would give other priorities less attention. This has to be the case, because as we all know by now, our government cannot indefinitely continue its practice of spending significantly more than it takes in. We must focus our efforts and our limited resources on the most important areas and be sure that our programs and policies are working.

At the bottom of the priority list we might find items like federal subsidies to sugar farmers, which are scheduled to total $1.4 billion between 2008 and 2017. Can we afford to continue these subsidies, which have been in place since the New Deal? More important, *should* the federal government be subsidizing what I call the "white tobacco," a leading contributor to our obesity epidemic? Let's all spell out the answer together: N-O. And there are plenty of other subsidies and programs that deserve the same answer.

A planning system would help make our government priorities and spending more transparent. This would improve government performance while also helping to better inform the public and reinvigorate our democracy.

As part of this process, we need to work from a common set of metrics that would give us a fact-based state of the union on demand. The federal government produces a plethora of powerful statistics about its operations and American life, but it's almost impossible for you and me to make sense of all the numbers. As comptroller general, beginning in 2003, I advocated that the government devise a set of key national indicators to plot our position and progress in areas such as the economy, the environment, health care, innovation, infrastructure, poverty, and security. We held a forum at the Government Accountability Office in partnership with the National Academy of Sciences. That effort spawned the State of the USA initiative. As I write this, a bipartisan effort to make this concept a reality and provide federal funding to create a related public-private partnership has begun in the U.S. Senate.

Under this plan, the National Academies would lead the effort to devise the indicators; take the federal data and the best information from state, private, and international sources; and display the information on a public website. The idea is to give Americans unimpeachable data on the state and progress of the country and our society. As former White House chief of staff Kenneth M. Duberstein wrote in *The New York Times:* "Imagine everyone having at their fingertips answers to questions like: How many quality jobs are we adding to the American economy? How many more students are getting into college? How many more people are gaining access to affordable health insurance? Are we increasing economic growth along with savings and investment? Are we reducing our greenhouse gas emissions?"

We all have issues that really matter to us, whether it's poverty or women's rights or economic growth. With reliable data to chart our progress in these areas, we could better understand the trends and what's working (and what's not). We citizens would be better informed and our elected representatives would be less able to pull the wool over our eyes. That's a formula for better government and a healthy democracy.

Determined citizens equipped with powerful information can accomplish a lot. Keep in mind that during the American Revolution, about one-third of the colonists supported the rebels, about one-third opposed them, and another third didn't care who won. A relatively small percentage of those who supported the Revolution took up arms or otherwise directly supported the effort—and they changed the world.

We twenty-first-century minutemen can do the same. Both the GAO and I continue to support establishing these key national indicators. After all, the GAO makes its living, in part, by auditing federal data and making sure all the numbers add up. The GAO's list of high-risk areas was intended above all to shine a light on government's performance. With light comes heat, and with heat comes action.

During my tenure as head of the GAO, I challenged the agency to practice what we preached and to lead by example—two of my favorite phrases. I'm pleased to say that the agency rose to the challenge. The balance of this chapter will outline some of the things we did, the results we achieved, and why it matters.

A MODEL FOR REFORM

A successful government agency has to have a clear mission, top talent, good systems for doing its job, and effective ways to measure whether it is doing that job as well as it should. Its employees should be motivated to work efficiently. Their work product should be plainly written and comprehensible. After all, government workers are paid by the taxpayers, and the taxpayers should be able to figure out what their employees are doing for that money.

Those government salaries are not so bad. It's true that public employees focus more on the rewards of their missions than on their paychecks. And it's true that people with excellent educations, highly marketable skills, and experience generally make more money in the private sector. But public employees do have some material advantages. Their jobs are more secure and their benefits more generous than most private workers enjoy, and economic cycles don't cause many ripples. The public is becoming increasingly aware of and concerned about this disconnect from reality.

That was true even in our recent severe recession. While private workers worried about pay cuts and layoffs, federal employees received across-the-board raises. As I write this, pending legislation would give federal employees pension credit for their unused sick leave. Once again, I have to wonder what planet Washington is on. Sick leave is supposed to be used when you're sick!

During my tenure, the GAO tried to preach sound values to the rest of the federal government. We did so as part of our essential mission: to serve as the investigative arm of Congress, auditing and evaluating government programs and activities. I came to office determined that we should, to repeat myself, lead by example and practice what we preached. We could make the GAO a model for how a federal agency should be run.

My motives were not completely altruistic. When I was sworn in as the seventh comptroller general of the United States and head of the GAO in November 1998, I knew we had to do our job better. I had a strong leadership team and a number of highly educated and dedicated professionals in place, but our numbers were shrinking.

The General Accounting Office (now the Government Accountability Office) was created in 1921 as part of the same law that created the Bureau of the Budget (now the Office of Management and Budget). The early GAO was focused on the review and approval of government vouchers before they were paid (preauditing). It used a type of red tape literally to bundle various approved vouchers for payment. The agency grew to over 15,000 at the height of World War II. Its role evolved after World War II to focus on postauditing, When Elmer Staats was comptroller general (1966 to 1981), he began the GAO's program evaluation function and expanded the GAO's international activities. Chuck Bowsher, who succeeded Elmer and served as comptroller general from 1981 to 1996, focused on improving federal financial management. He also oversaw the GAO's efforts during the savings and loan fiasco.

During my tenure as comptroller general (1998 to 2008), I focused the GAO's efforts on a range of oversight, insight, and foresight activities. We sought to capitalize on the agency's competitive advantages and to lead by example in our efforts to transform the government and the accountability profession both domestically and internationally. I also championed federal fiscal responsibility and accountability as comptroller general.

In the three years before I took office, the GAO's total staff had been cut by nearly 40 percent. That happened after the Republicans had captured control of both houses of Congress for the first time in forty years. GOP leaders wanted to cut the size of government on principle, and focused in particular on the GAO, which was the biggest agency attached to the Congress and which they felt, rightly or wrongly, had become a tool of the Democratic leadership. Finally, the new Republican leaders questioned the value of some of the GAO's work and felt that it had become too focused on its own agenda rather than on the needs and interests of the Congress. A survey of Republican House members showed that they favored cutting the agency even further. A number of senators felt the same way.

In short, the GAO was on a burning platform, and it needed to engage in some dramatic and fundamental changes. I had to move boldly to show these doubting members of Congress that the GAO could be an essential, independent tool of government performance, accountability, and transformational reform. Fortunately, "transformation" is my middle name (well, not really), and I had the freedom to act decisively. My job as comptroller general came with a fifteen-year term, the longest of any in the federal government other than judges who receive lifetime appointments. Furthermore, the comptroller general can be removed from office only by impeachment or joint resolution of Congress, and only for specific reasons. These factors gave me a much greater degree of independence and job security than a typical agency head would enjoy. When one party controls the Senate, the House, and the White House, the comptroller general is one of only a very few officials who can speak truth to power without fear of personal reprisal.

Shortly after starting my job, I addressed all GAO employees, telling them the three main objectives I hoped to achieve during my tenure. They were: (1) to transform the GAO into an agency that led by example and practiced what it preached; (2) to help transform the accountability profession so that it could better meet the challenges and capitalize on the opportunities of the twenty-first century; and (3) to help the federal government make a down payment on its huge unfunded obligations and begin to transform how it does business.

During the almost ten years that followed, I learned that in making tough transformations, you go from patience to persistence to perseverance to pain before you prevail. I knew where I wanted to take the agency, but I had to work issue by issue to get it there.

While I was still getting used to my chair, several GAO executives briefed me on the agency's efforts to prepare the government's computers for the year 2000 conversion. The GAO had done a huge amount of work for the Congress on this issue and had issued many reports and recommendations. When I was briefed on these efforts, I asked one simple question: Had our team reviewed our own internal efforts on Y2K and had we adopted all of the applicable recommendations we had made to others? Stated differently, were we leading by example and practicing what we preached? Unfortunately, as the look on the GAO executives' faces told me, the answer was no. This provided me with the perfect opportunity to make my case, which I did then and many times afterward.

As I learned more about our operations, I was very surprised to find out that while the GAO had existed since 1921, it had never developed an agency-wide strategic, integrated, and forward-looking plan to guide its actions, allocate its resources, and measure its results. In my view, if you don't have a plan you don't have a prayer to maximize your value and mitigate your risk. Therefore, we began to put one together, and that made a huge difference in improving our performance. In fairness to the GAO, as you found out a few pages ago, the U.S. government as a whole has never had such a strategic plan, and it has existed for more than 220 years.

We needed more than a plan. We also had to develop transparent protocols to guide our work. Achieving clear working guidelines helped reduce complaints in Congress and the executive branch that the GAO was treating some unfairly.

Most important of all, we had to pull ourselves together as an agency with a common resolve. Shortly after starting at the GAO, I brought the top executives together to gain agreement on a set of core values that would serve as a foundation of our work. We finally agreed on three: accountability, integrity, and reliability. These words appeared over our entrance doors, on our business cards, and in all key publications of the agency.

Accountability described what we did—audits, investigations, program evaluations, legal adjudications, and other things. Integrity described how we performed our work—in a professional, objective, fact-based, nonpartisan, nonideological, fair, and balanced manner. Reliability described how we wanted our work to be received—as timely, accurate, useful, clear, and candid. We talked about these three values so much that they became a kind of acronym—AIR—and, of course, people started calling me "Air Walker" (although I'm confident that "Air Jordan" is not particularly concerned about this challenge).

I actually had one concern even more basic than our values. From early in my tenure, I didn't like our name—"General Accounting Office." It did not reflect what the agency did, and that caused confusion among members of Congress, cabinet officials, and job candidates. Many people thought the agency was made up mainly of accountants focused on financial auditing. These perceptions were very far from the truth. In fact, only about 15 percent of the GAO's staff and work had to do with traditional financial auditing. We spent most of our efforts assessing the effectiveness of government programs and completing other congressional assignments.

I decided to push for a change in the agency's name, after an appropriate period of time had passed. The adoption of the term "accountability" as our first core value aided my effort. As a result, in 2004, and at my request, the Congress passed and the president signed legislation that included a number of human capital and other reforms and changed the name of the General Accounting Office to the U.S. Government Accountability Office. This let us keep the brand name, which was, is, and should remain GAO.

Before worrying about our name, we set off to demonstrate that the leaner, meaner GAO could operate much more efficiently and effectively than much larger federal agencies. By the time I took my job, the agency already had gone from more than forty field offices to sixteen. I toured all sixteen, then cut the number to eleven. I believed that we should minimize the number of our layers, silos, and footprints in order to maximize flexibility and accountability. In addition, I wanted to put these office closures behind us and promised that there would be no more during my tenure unless we ran into serious budgetary constraints.

I expected to get a lot of blowback from senators and members of Congress whose states lost jobs because of these office closures. Fortunately, we did not, in large part because of an extensive outreach effort with key congressional leaders and the affected congressional offices to explain what we were proposing to do and why we needed to do it.

We also restructured. We reduced the number of organizational units from thirty-five "Issue Areas," relating to a number of fairly narrowly focused subject areas, to thirteen "Teams," relating to a broader range of key subject areas (such as defense, health care, physical infrastructure, and acquisitions). And we eliminated a layer of senior management without laying off a single person. The moves were merit based and designed to match each individual's skills with the GAO's institutional needs. We didn't just eliminate positions; we also created flexible new units to manage quality control, strategic planning, external liaisons, equal opportunity, and other GAO-wide functions.

Since we were in the performance and accountability business, we worked to develop a balanced set of measures to assess our own overall performance. We focused on our results, our people, our clients, and our external partners. Historically, the GAO had used the number of reports that it generated as a performance metric. The culture favored a very thick "Chapter Report," even if it took years to produce and had little impact. I challenged that culture.

Our new performance metrics focused on things like the number of recommendations that we made, the percentage of our recommendations that were adopted within a reasonable period of time (generally four years), the financial benefits that accrued from adopting our recommendations, and other benefits that could not be translated into monetary terms.

You won't be surprised to learn that our efforts to change how we worked were not as challenging as our efforts to reform how our staff was organized, evaluated, and paid. This was not only a touchy topic but a vitally important one, since human capital represented about 80 percent of our agency's budget.

We set out to dramatically reform the agency's performance appraisal system, which had tended to give everybody high marks. We installed a dramatically different system, in which the average employee rating fell from 4.62 to 2.19 out of 5. In the old system, 20 percent of our employees had received a perfect 5.0; in the new reviews, only 2 percent earned perfect marks. This caused some obvious concerns among staff members, who found out for the first time how they were ranked in their peer group. As time went on, we began to tie a portion of our employees' pay to our new performance appraisal system. That's when we started to hear some grumbling from the ranks.

Then came by far the biggest single human capital challenge during my tenure. We restructured the GAO's mid-level professional staff to help promote the principle of equal pay for equal work. I am a big believer in that concept—and in ensuring that pay systems are competitive, affordable, and sustainable. In my view, the existing system was not only inequitable, but it resulted in excess compensation being paid to a large number of senior auditors and analysts, among others. While these were good people who were performing at an acceptable level or above, they did not have supervisory or other highly specialized responsibilities that justified their pay range. In fact, because of the way the GAO's classification and pay systems had been structured in the late 1980s, nonsupervisory senior auditors or analysts could be paid more than an assistant director two tiers higher. This made no sense to me and it didn't pass a straight-face test when you discussed it with the general public.

As we set out to unscramble the egg, we promised that no one's pay would be cut, even if it was significantly in excess of prevailing market levels. At the same time, some of those overpaid employees might see their pay frozen for a period of time. Many employees were not happy with this change, even some who were not affected by it. As a result of this mid-level restructuring, a portion of the GAO's workforce joined a union. A lot of people thought I would be upset about that, but I wasn't. Both of my grandfathers were union members, and one was head of his union local. Having a union represent these employees actually made it easier to deal with some issues, although it was tougher to deal with others.

The GAO's human capital transformations, even the controversial mid-level restructuring, were eventually put in place. In my view, it was better to complete these transformations quickly rather than wait and possibly never get them implemented. Furthermore, once the new rules are in place, any changes have to be negotiated.

In fact, all the transformational reforms outlined in this chapter were achieved employing the incentives, transparency, and accountability concepts discussed earlier in this book. They have all

	1998	2008
Total personnel (full-time equivalent)	3,500	3,081
Total budget (in 2008 dollars)	$481.4 million	$529.6 million
Number of field offices	16	11
Number of mission units	35	13
Layers of executive management below comptroller general	3	2
Financial benefits	$19.7 billion	$58.1 billion
Return on investment per dollar of budget	$53	$110
Return on investment per employee (full-time equivalent)	$5.6 million	$18.9 million
Nonfinancial benefits (resulting from GAO recommendations)	537	1,398
Percentage of reports with recommendations	untracked	66%
Percentage of recommendations adopted/implemented	untracked	83%
Client satisfaction rating	untracked	98%
Federal Employee Feedback Ranking	n/a	2

Figure 11 Progress of the Government Accountability Office. At the GAO, we sought to lead by example and show that transformation is possible in government.

survived my tenure and are likely to stay in place for many years. The bottom line is that despite an approximate 12 percent reduction in the GAO's personnel, the agency's results improved dramatically across the board. For example, financial benefits per GAO employee more than tripled, and the overall return for each budget dollar invested in the agency more than doubled. The numbers speak for themselves. They are clear and compelling. (See figure 11.) These results were achieved through a true team effort, and everyone involved can take pride in the achievements. In particular, the GAO's executive committee, which I chaired, and which included Gene Dodaro, Tony Gamboa, Gary Kepplinger, and Sallyanne Harper during most of my tenure, deserves special recognition. Many other GAO executives and employees also contributed to our collective success.

While the GAO is not a huge agency, our efforts demonstrate that real transformation is possible in the federal government. The reforms we accomplished at the GAO are scalable and transferable to other agencies. Hopefully, they will be adopted in time.

So far, we have talked about policy changes and, in this chapter, the transformation in processes we need to make. But there's one more chapter left, fellow citizens. It's time to talk about our role—what "We the People" must do to transform our political system into one that works for our collective best interest. Yes, we'll also be called upon to remember our civics lessons about changing the Constitution.

Eleven

FIXING OUR DYSFUNCTIONAL DEMOCRACY

How can we go about overhauling our broken government and the bad policies it produces? Good question, especially the "we" part.

We can start by demanding more truth, transparency, foresight, and accountability from the policy makers who are responsible for the key issues facing our nation. We can also push for major policy and operational reforms, along with the processes that will be necessary to help ensure that they are implemented. We can do all of this and more within our political system. But we also need to repair the American political system, and I'll show you how.

First we have to recognize who let our system decay: You and I did. The Constitution gives us citizens the power to choose the people who will represent us and who will lead our government, and, frankly, we have not been doing a great job. You and I are the ones who elected and continue to reelect those partisan bickerers, magic practitioners, and professional politicians who dominate

Washington. Now we have to recognize something else: You and I also can change things, and we should start now.

We have the power. I'm publishing this book at the start of 2010 for good reason. Last year we were obsessed by the emergency steps needed to address our housing and financial crises and to pull us out of the recession that resulted. That's still not all behind us, of course, but now is a time for chastened new beginnings, to look ahead and to start taking steps to help create a better future for our nation. We have to act responsibly, because we've recently seen what happens when people are not responsible.

There's only one way to reform a system that will not reform itself, and that's to form a citizens' action movement and instigate a grassroots effort to change the status quo within Washington's Beltway. So here's your invitation. Onward, soldiers of the sensible center!

The Peterson Foundation, which I lead, is joining forces with like-minded groups across the nation to build a critical mass of public opinion in favor of saving our future. We all have our separate agendas, but we are all committed to making sure that elected officials start making tough choices before we pass a tipping point and inflict irreparable damage on our country's future and its place in the world. We don't need a huge national majority to prevail. We need you—and a growing group of committed individuals who will make enough noise to force Washington to listen, and to act.

As I've emphasized throughout this book, there are no magical answers—only commonsense solutions requiring commitment and lots of hard work. I'm talking about the kind of work Ross Perot did to make sure that the country adopted a more sound fiscal policy in the 1990s. He didn't perform any magic. He simply told the truth about our nation's deteriorating financial condition and put the facts in front of us, where we couldn't ignore them.

That's what we have to do today. If we can put the facts before enough people, we will gather the support we need to start a process leading to real reform. After all, things are much worse now than they were then.

First, let's diagnose why we need a citizen's movement apart from our supposedly representative government. According to the textbooks, our elected officials should be working for our best interest. Tell me, now that you've read most of this book, do you think they have done that? For example, is it in our nation's best interest to slide ever deeper into debt and to become ever more dependent on foreign lenders? You know my answer to that one. So what's gone wrong with our politicians?

Like most people with good jobs, they want to keep theirs. From day one of their terms, most have a firm eye on the day when voters will decide whether to reelect them, and of course a whole industry of "experts" has arisen around packaging them for reelection. It's not surprising in this context that they promise to raise your benefits while cutting your taxes. That promise doesn't make sense, does it? You and I both know that it doesn't, and yet it has worked spectacularly for any number of politicians over the years, to the great detriment of our country.

When representatives elected on that platform reach office in Washington, they are primed to vote for short-term advantage (more social benefits) and long-term disaster (insufficient revenues). Politicians who earn their keep on one side or the other of that equation create the warring factions that have made our Congress a nightmare of partisan battles and ideological divides rather than a sounding board for honest debate and sensible-center solutions.

Sometimes these politicians are even asked to sign "pledges" to vote according to the correct ideological line on tax and benefits issues. That puts these representatives in the position of having to make absolute commitments before they even know the facts of an issue. Is that any way to conduct a public debate?

If you look at the logic prevalent in Washington, you can come to only one conclusion: We have a dysfunctional democracy.

And so we must talk about how to change our politics, and that's probably the biggest and most fundamental change we'll need to make in the years ahead. Partisan battles and ideological divides helped get us into this mess, but they won't help get us out. Nor will bipartisanship, a concept that is outdated, because it still focuses too much on existing political parties and not enough on the country as a whole. Several polls have shown that a plurality of Americans (including me) now consider ourselves to be political independents. If you seek only bipartisan solutions, you are excluding all of us. What we need now is nonpartisanship.

You'll get the drift of that as you read along. At the heart of this strategy is the elemental American effort to build a popular movement. Beyond creating a critical mass of public opinion, we can use this movement to support mechanisms that will be guaranteed to put needed reforms before Congress.

I won't stop there. Now that I have your attention, I'm going to be very free and easy about putting other major political changes on our agenda for discussion—including constitutional changes. My proposals may sound a bit, well, idealistic. We Americans have always been leery of amending our Constitution. But let me tell you this: It's time to think in dramatic and transformational ways.

I will concede at the top that I don't expect an ambitious constitutional convention to meet anytime soon. But I do know from my Washington experience that even the first rumblings about the need for dramatic and fundamental change, coming from a sizable number of Americans, will attract close attention in the capital. These politicians are professionals, after all, and it's their job to try and stay ahead of political shifts. So let's start rumbling.

HOW OUR POLITICS EVOLVED

Step one is to remember who we are. It took leaders, not laggards, to forge our nation's identity and strength. It took hard work, prudence, thrift, saving, and personal responsibility—and the old-fashioned American desire to avoid too much debt—to make us the strongest economic power on earth. And most of all it took our sense of stewardship, a commitment dating from our origins in an untamed land, to always strive to pass on a better country to the next generation of Americans.

Our Constitution created American politics, and we were lucky that George Washington was selected to be our first president. He did not pursue the office, yet in assuming it he defined the role.

At the time, the prevailing view was that the ideal president, like Washington, would be a reluctant soldier—a farmer, professional man, or merchant who would be called to duty from a life other than politics. He would govern all Americans and be respected by his fellow citizens. He would wield appropriate authority. If people had the right to form their government, they had the corresponding duty to obey it. Factionalism was a sin and politics was an evil.

General Washington (he preferred that title to "President") reviled the very idea of political parties. "They serve to organize faction, to give it an artificial and extraordinary force," he said in his farewell address, "to put, in the place of the delegated will of the nation, the will of a party, often a small but artful and enterprising minority of the community."

Sorry, General. Washington's dream of a government linked to the people by a common culture and their recognition of a common good while shunning formal political parties didn't last very long. His successor, John Adams, had apprenticed in Massachusetts politics, shepherded the Declaration of Independence, and served as a diplomat and as Washington's vice president before taking the presidency himself. Yes, he was a farmer, but he was also very much a political pro.

Not only that, Adams was a lawyer (as were half the men who signed the Declaration of Independence). Adams's presidency, no less than Washington's, marked the beginning of America's governmental tradition. The culture of the lawyer took root quickly in our nation's capital, to the consternation of nonlawyers like Adams's rival, Thomas Jefferson. "If the present Congress errs in too much talking," Jefferson wrote, "how can it be otherwise in a body to which the people send one hundred and fifty lawyers, whose trade it is to question everything, yield nothing, and talk by the hour?"

Jefferson would still be complaining today. So far in our history, twenty-six of our forty-four presidents have been lawyers. And in numbers, lawyers have been by far the most plentiful members of our legislative branch. When the 111th Congress convened in early 2009, 54 percent of the senators and 36 percent of the House members present were lawyers.

Their prevalence has helped shape Washington's culture. There are good lawyers, of course, just as there are good politicians, and the practice of law has an honored and vital role in our society. My point is that lawyers exemplify the politicians in our leadership who typically lack experience in the real world. Professional politicians, like the professional lawyers many of them are, take office with very little experience in the practical pursuits of their constituents—manufacturing things, inventing things, transporting people and products, caring for the ill, and teaching young people.

If politicians rank rather low on the list of esteemed professionals in America, that is partly because lawyers do, too. But mostly, it's because many people don't consider them to be part of the mainstream of America.

Most Americans see themselves as problem-solvers and doers, and often they see lawyers as nitpickers and naysayers. Like lawyers, lawmakers have a language of their own. That's the special language of our nation's capital—I've been introducing it to you here and there in this book. These Washington words are another of the factors that separate people inside Washington's Beltway from the rest of us.

THE INCUMBENCY DISEASE

That language can flourish because the culture that nurtures it is not only isolated but self-preserving. The politicians, aides, lobbyists, consultants, and others who occupy and influence the center of national power are pros who have worked together for years, often decades. Yes, we have elections every couple of years, but the political process has become so adept at protecting incumbents that for most sitting members of Congress, running for office amounts to little but a periodic pain in the keister. (That's a sophisticated southern term.)

Just look at the numbers. Since the end of World War II, according to a study by the Constitutional Rights Foundation, U.S. senators have won reelection 75 percent of the time. And they're less secure than House members, who have won reelection 90 percent of the time.

Even the newcomers tend to be insiders. Over the years, most of those entering Congress for the first time are experienced politicians, defined as individuals who have won elections at other levels of government. The sad truth is that a shrinking minority are amateurs in the "Mr. Smith Goes to Washington" tradition. I congratulate all the newcomers for climbing the ladder from local councils to Washington. Their skills took them far. But the arrival of this nonstop stream of political pros exacerbates the problem we have in promoting real-world leaders to national politics.

This largely holds true even in times of upheaval, when Americans vote to "throw the rascals out." In the 1994 Republican revolution, when the GOP swept to control of Congress, only 45 percent of the new House members had never held office before, and only half of the new senators. So much for fresh faces.

No matter what the state of the country, no matter how angry the voters, the Washington establishment marches along to its own cadence, which is increasingly out of touch with reality. This insular culture is one big reason our nation's capital always seems to be reacting to crises rather than addressing our challenges head-on.

Washington is a lagging indicator on just about everything. Yes, Washington is a lag indicator and the Congress is a lag indicator within Washington. The truth is that if the Congress is taking on some societal illness, you can be certain that the poor patient is close to death. If members of Congress were on a pay-for-performance plan, many would owe us money!

THE FAILURE OF PARTY POLITICS

Which party happens to hold power at any given time matters a lot when it comes to dividing up the spoils—but not so much when it comes to combating the huge fiscal problems I've been describing. Occasionally our two political parties reach accord and celebrate their "bipartisanship." But bipartisanship is no cure-all when it comes to the really big challenges facing our country.

For most of the time since 1945, we haven't been able to blame solely the Democrats or the Republicans for our failed fiscal policies. The facts show that both parties have been responsible for our state of affairs. During most of the years since 1945, the Democrats dominated the House and only a bit less so the Senate, while the trend favored Republicans in the White House. For fifty of the sixty-four years between 1945 and 2009, no one party controlled all three centers of political power—namely, the Senate, the House, and the White House.

When you look at some of the most important stages in our fiscal downfall, the message becomes clear: The whole establishment was to blame. Throughout the 1980s, when Republican president Reagan's tax cuts and defense spending increased our fiscal challenges, Democrats controlled at least one house of Congress every step of the way.

The parties share the blame for the red ink in our nation's entitlement programs. The Democrats controlled both houses of Congress when President Johnson signed the Medicare law in 1965, and the Republicans controlled both houses of Congress when President Bush 43 signed the new Medicare prescription drug benefit into law just a few years ago.

On the other side of the coin, the Democrats controlled at least one house when President Bush 41 took steps to address the growing budget deficit, and the Republicans controlled both houses during most of the time Democrat Clinton was taking steps to balance the budget.

In any event, it's clear that no pattern of righteousness emerges here. In fact, in my view, while individual members of Congress are fiscally responsible, there is no party of fiscal responsibility. They tend to get more serious about this subject when they are out of power than they do when they are in charge.

If bipartisanship hasn't helped in recent times, outright partisanship has made things worse. Partisanship widens the large and growing ideological divide that obstructs progress in Washington. A stalemate in our nation's capital is not all bad when things are going well. After all, sometimes Congress can muck things up. However, having a stalemate when things are not going well—and getting worse—is unacceptable and it needs to be addressed.

Our election system seems almost to guarantee that this ideological divide will continue. In all but a handful of states such as Arizona and Iowa, state legislatures draw the boundaries of congressional districts. Thanks to modern computer technology, the parties in control have become expert at custom-designing the districts to protect their parties and incumbents on a block-by-block level in every town. As a result, only about 60 of our 435 congressional seats are considered truly competitive. The overwhelming majority of seats are safe for the party in control and for the incumbents in office.

If incumbents face any real challenge at all, it is in their party primaries, when a party's most ideological supporters tend to turn out. In a primary, a Democratic incumbent will feel pressure from the left, and a Republican from the right. Over time, that pushes both parties to their extremes and turns Washington's political debates into ideological noise fests. Our political system is well designed to create television talking heads and "fact-free zones," public shouting matches, and legislative gridlock—but not so great at representing the needs of most Americans or at making progress on their behalf.

The way districts are custom-designed explains why so many Americans like their local Congress member. He or she is probably a pro who knows how to bring home the bacon and reflects the ideological majority of the district's activists (even if those policy stances vary considerably from the more centrist views of the nation). But the workings of the system also explain why so many Americans hold such a low opinion of Congress as a whole.

Congress is a model of the dysfunction I'm writing about. Like the Pentagon, it needs to reduce its bureaucracy—in this case, the plethora of committees and subcommittees—and take a more integrated approach to its duties. Right now, inefficiency is the name of the game. More than twenty Senate and House committees claim jurisdiction over the relatively new Department of Homeland Security, for example. This is not productive for the department, the Congress, or the American people.

Congressional dysfunction is the political underpinning of our fiscal crisis. Too many Republicans won't retreat from promoting lower taxes and smaller government. Too many Democrats refuse to restructure our unsustainable social insurance contracts, and insist on advocating a larger and more activist government. That leaves us with both low taxes and unsustainable benefit programs, even though these policies are putting us in the poorhouse. Here's the independent view: We don't need either a "small government" or a "big government." We need an effective government—one that is fiscally responsible, focuses on the future, and looks out for the collective best interest of America and Americans rather than the narrow agendas of various special interests.

There is little room for compromise in the ideological wars. It's getting harder to find a conservative Democrat anymore, or a moderate Republican (although some of these rare birds still exist). It's even harder to find the sensible center on key issues facing our society. For independents like me and a growing plurality of Americans, there may be no place at the table at all.

It will be hard to change that. The formula of low taxes and generous social spending that has created this disaster will be hard to eliminate. For the past few decades, our political culture has played to what divides us rather than what unites us. Politicians pit us against each other in the great grab for goodies. They have often reduced this voraciousness to specious cries for "fairness." They tell us that adding benefits is "fair" to those who get them. They also tell us that raising taxes on anyone but the "rich" to pay for government is "unfair," because "hardworking" taxpayers should be able to keep more of their "hard-earned" money.

This is a lethal political formula. Just look at what happens to our national leaders who choose a different way. Bush 41, as a recent example, became associated with tax increases and lost reelection for doing the fiscally responsible thing. His son, Bush 43, the tax cutter, entitlement expander, and father of preemptive wars, on the other hand, won two terms despite the fact that our deficit and debt levels exploded during his administration.

Now it is President Obama's turn. His promise to add a huge new national health care program while not raising taxes on anyone making less than $250,000 a year sounds like the same old get-something-for-nothing marketing pitch we have been hearing from politicians for decades. Don't worry, everybody, I'm going to ladle out lots of new benefits and only the "rich" will pay. What kind of "change" is that?

The higher base level of federal spending from Obama's 2009 budget, his first signed budget bill, will be with us long after the recession ends. And what will we get for it? If history is any guide, not much, other than higher taxes and fewer choices.

Will Obama eventually see the light and move toward a more limited, responsive, results-oriented, and fiscally responsible government? And will he make the transition from campaign mode (in which he's greatly overexposed) to governing mode—in which he will act on rather than just talk about fiscal responsibility? I sure hope so.

FACING UP TO REFORM

As you have read this book, I've been showing you that solutions in the sensible center can avoid both taxes that are too high and government benefits that are too expansive. There can be a commonsense solution to every problem. If you look back over the remedies I'm suggesting for Social Security, health care, taxes, defense, and other issues, you can boil down my approach to three questions: What do we need as a nation, what can we afford, and how can we best pay for it?

As individuals, we do the best we can for ourselves and our families. As a nation, we do what's best for our country for both today and tomorrow. Those who receive government benefits must see that adjustments are sometimes necessary—such as raising the eligibility age for Social Security. A step like that is not "unfair"; it is simply a recognition that Americans are living longer than they did in 1935, when Social Security was created, and that our economy has switched from an industrial base to a service base. We need Americans to work until a later age not just for fiscal reasons, but also to keep our economic growth strong during a time when our workforce is shrinking.

Those of us paying taxes and fees to support government benefits should see that we are helping ourselves with our contributions. Those who can afford to pay more should pay more, both in taxes and in premiums for voluntary government programs like some of Medicare's. That is not a socialist concept; it's a common-sense concept. But there is a limit as to how much they should be required to pay.

All of this is easy to say, but it will be tough to accomplish. On the policy front, it will take something like the Fiscal Future Commission I proposed earlier in this book to help us jump-start the major policy reforms that are needed. The commission would recommend reforms in how the federal government handles budgeting, distributes government benefits, and levies taxes. These recommendations would not sit on a shelf as so many others have. Congress—by law—would vote these measures up or down.

In addition to a Fiscal Future Commission, we need a separate group of transformational leaders to get government to focus more on results and to properly align the federal government with the realities of the twenty-first century. If handled correctly, the Baseline Review Commission (or Government Transformation Commission) I proposed in the previous chapter could be as effective as the Hoover Commission in Truman's time. Truman used that independent commission to streamline the workings of the executive branch, and the Congress ultimately adopted most of the commission's proposed reforms. The new commission I am suggesting would help to transform our government priorities, preparing us for leadership in the twenty-first century, and would help improve the federal government's economy, efficiency, effectiveness, credibility, and accountability.

Only extraordinary commissions like these will be in a position to state the facts, speak the truth, and take the heat from championing the long-overdue reforms we need. By their very existence, they will make clear to Americans that it is not a question of whether budget controls, entitlement changes, tax reforms, and other transformational changes will be made; it's only a matter of which ones and when.

You're familiar with my proposals in these areas by now. This is mostly a policy book after all. But as we approach the last few pages, let me suggest that we may need more than changes in government policies and practices to secure our collective future, strengthen our democracy, and save our republic.

The bottom line is that to change the kinds of damaging policies our system produces, we might have to change the system itself. And it might take constitutional amendments to do that. Again, I know this is not the most practical suggestion in this book. However, I can imagine a number of serious reforms that could be achieved by amending the Constitution through a grassroots effort. Even if the effort ultimately fails, it will send a message to our elected officials, and may just encourage them to act.

Amending our Constitution is not something to take lightly. There are only two ways to do it, both arduous. In the method we've used in the past, both houses of Congress approve the amendment by two-thirds majorities, after which three-fourths of the state legislatures (or conventions called by the states) must ratify the change.

In a second process, which has never been used, two-thirds of the state legislatures (or state conventions) call for a national constitutional convention, and any measure approved by the national body must be approved by three-fourths of the state legislatures or conventions.

You will notice that the second option bypasses Washington's political establishment entirely. That's never been tried. Some argue that a national constitutional convention might open a Pandora's box and approve who-knows-what changes (although its work would still have to be ratified by three-fourths of the states). But imagine if we simply started a serious national effort to call for such a convention to address a number of specific, predetermined, and agreed-upon issues—and imagine a few large and influential state legislatures going along. Do you think we would get Washington's attention? I do.

What are some of the issues a constitutional convention would take on? We could find many constructive ideas among the states (as our founders intended). We should look at how Arizona and Iowa draw up their congressional districts, for example, using nonpartisan redistricting commissions rather than partisan state legislatures. And we should look at Maine's popular formula for financing elections for state office with public funds.

We could also boost the sensible center in presidential elections by changing the way we allocate Electoral College votes. Most states award all of their votes to the candidate who wins that state. But why not award most of the votes according to who wins each congressional district, and then give the winner of the state the two electoral votes associated with its Senate seats? That would force presidential candidates to court more than just a few big swing states. It could make a big difference in close elections. If this rule had been in effect in 2000 and 2004, the results might have been different.

(A constitutional amendment is not technically necessary for changing how electoral votes are allocated. Nebraska already apportions its Electoral College votes the way I described above. However, as in the case of the redistricting issue, a constitutional effort would accelerate change.)

We could, of course, eliminate this Electoral College confusion entirely. We could change to a popular vote for electing our president and vice president. That change would definitely require a change to the Constitution.

We should also give ordinary voters more clout by reforming policies on financing campaigns with private money. For one thing, we could place limits on the ability of wealthy candidates to funnel millions of dollars of their own money into their own campaigns. We could also require that a supermajority (say, 80 percent) of candidates' contributions come from actual constituents. Candidates could still take money from political action committees or distant fat cats, but they would be required to rely primarily on contributions from real people, other than themselves, who live in and can vote in their districts.

Does it look like I want to make it tougher for people to make a career out of politics, especially those who serve in the same job for many years? You got that right. Which brings me to the subject of term limits. In my view, we should have them, since the positives outweigh the negatives. This reform would clearly require a constitutional amendment.

We need to learn from the experiences of some states and make sure that the limits we impose aren't too short. If you give politicians a four- to six-year term limit, they will have to start figuring out what they want to run for next almost as soon as they're elected. The rapid turnover also will increase the power of behind-the-scenes staff members, who, no matter how capable and dedicated they may be, aren't elected by anybody and aren't directly accountable to the people. I would suggest twelve- to eighteen-year term limits. That tells an aspiring politician: Sure, you can have a political career—just not all in the same job.

Speaking of terms, we should give members of the House of Representatives four-year terms of office (instead of the present two) and hold elections for half of the House every two years. We should also consider having the president serve one six- to eight-year term. That way, these politicians wouldn't be running for a second term from day one. After all, we always have impeachment if they really mess up.

Changes like the ones outlined in this chapter would make our politicians more responsive and responsible, but we also have to give them a constraint to force more prudent behavior once they do assume elective office. That is, there should be a constitutional limit on the extent to which Washington can mortgage our nation's and families' futures.

PUT A LIMIT ON DEBT

The issue that we really need to address is not balancing the short-term federal budget so much as it is controlling our growing structural deficits—caused by those programs on autopilot—and our escalating debt levels. We must take both mandatory spending programs and tax preferences off autopilot if we want to avoid flying into a mountain of debt. A constitutional amendment could require the federal government to limit total debt to, say, no more than 125 percent of GDP (three percentage points higher than our all-time record at the end of World War II), absent a declaration of war or some unforeseeable financial calamity like a depression or serious recession.

At present our total debt adds up to almost 85 percent of GDP and, based on projections by the Congressional Budget Office, it's expected to climb to almost 95 percent by the end of 2010. If the limit I proposed were in effect, there would still be some room for more borrowing—but there would also be a clear credit card limit. After all, there should be a limit on how much of other people's money elected officials can spend, especially if those other people aren't even born yet.

While we are at it, we should have an amendment stating that all federal spending should have a national purpose. We would give the president a line-item veto to enforce it. Right now, the president has to veto either an entire bill or nothing. So when Congress gives him a bill he can't veto—providing financing for the Afghanistan war, for example—members of Congress may tack on lots of goodies for themselves. Maybe Congressman Benevolent will order up a new library, federal building, or bridge back home named after himself. If the president had a line-item veto, he could approve the war financing while curbing our generosity to the memory of Congressman Benevolent. Come on, Ben, can't it wait at least until you've passed on?

We need to take additional steps to help ensure knowledge of and compliance with our nation's Constitution. In this regard, every member of Congress, along with every other legislative, executive, and judicial branch official who is required to take an oath to support and defend the Constitution, should be required to pass an annual exam on its details. Maybe we could hold an exam on Constitution Day, September 17. And to help ensure that all parties take it seriously, the results would be made public.

Call me a dreamer, but even spreading the word about a few major political reforms like these would be powerful enough to stir up some storm clouds over the heads of the ruling class in Washington and might start generating some real reforms. I spent almost ten years working for the Congress in Washington auditing, analyzing, and testifying about a broad range of federal government policy and operational issues. My position gave me access to the inner workings of that machinery without being part of anybody's "team." And what I saw convinced me that the best path to real reform must start beyond Washington's Beltway.

What Washington really needs if it is to work better is not a new president or a new budget plan. It's you and me, "We the People." We Americans, acting as shareholders of our nation (and treating it like a family business), can re-adopt the values and principles that made us great and take the steps necessary to ensure that our collective future will be better than our past.

Trust me, there is still time to change things. Will you help? If you and I join with others, we can make America the comeback country and extend the vitality of our republic far into the future. In the end, Washington is a mirror of our society. It will reflect the values and priorities that we demand of it.

Epilogue

Are you feeling fired up yet? At the start of this book, I pointed out that you had just committed yourself to absorbing several-score pages on the subject of America's looming fiscal crisis and certain other key sustainability challenges. In ordinary times, that is one of those worthy topics that everybody knows is important but nobody wants to read about. In the course of most Americans' lives, worrying about such major, mind-boggling challenges ranks right up there with worrying about the Mideast crisis—a perennial pastime best left to others.

So let me say at the start of this little epilogue: Thank you. When you picked up this book, you knew you weren't buying a light read for the beach—or a typical Washington tell-all full of espionage, sex scandals, war planning, and gladiators jousting in the political arena. Instead, you took on a serious book about significant challenges facing our government and country. This is the inside world of Washington, where people ride to work on the Metro every day and operate the machinery that governs America. This isn't a story of White House intrigue or high-level gamesmanship. It's a story about the malfunctioning of the great machine itself.

In the world of this book, it matters less who wins the struggle for political power and policy dominance. What matters is that at the present time no powerful player or political party has been able to take up the mantle to halt our national slide toward bankruptcy. This plotline will not end in a satisfying climax and denouement. It will take us slowly, sometimes imperceptibly, but inexorably toward the erosion of the American lifestyle and the diminution of America's standing in the world, unless we turn things around. And it will take a lot of work to do that. There's no easy resolution or happily-ever-after scenario at the end of this book.

Except one: You have read it, and hopefully, you will recommend it and share its many messages with others. When our Founding Fathers broke our ties with England and set America on its independent course, they reached for freedom not only from the king's control but from the mother country's traditions, dominated by elites and noblesse oblige and all the intrigues of court. In America, things would be different. People would govern through representatives who stood for all of their interests. The founders trusted us—they trusted you—to govern according to the broad needs of the citizenry rather than pursue the perquisites and special interests of the few. That's democracy American-style, by way of our Constitution and political values.

In reading this book, you have put your own hands on the levers of our government. I hope you find my case compelling, and I hope you buy into many of the illustrative solutions I have proposed. But what is really important is that you have grabbed those levers and hopefully will not let go. By doing that, you can begin to exercise power the American way. And that's our best hope for repairing the road to our future.

This book has covered more than our political culture. I have tried in these pages, as I did in my government service, to revive what I can only call the pragmatic idealism of the American way in order to keep the American Dream alive. From the start of our national story, when we set out to develop a continent and build a nation, we adopted the values of industry and thrift as emblematic of our economic lives. Not every American has a Horatio Alger or Peter G. Peterson story, but we all respect the stories of the citizens such as these who achieve success and wealth through their own enterprise and hard work. Pete Peterson was born to a very poor Greek immigrant family, and through the good education they provided him and by working hard he rose to lead major entities in government and industry and on Wall Street. He's now a billionaire who puts his money where his mouth is and his effort where his heart lies. In many ways, Pete is a case study in the American Dream come true.

Pete's kind of success through striving and sacrifice has largely become a national myth. It doesn't make pleasant reading for me to point out that too many Americans today are reaching not for the opportunity to maximize their own potential but for government benefits delivered at the least possible personal cost.

That reflects the central breakdown of our government: the impetus to provide services without adequately paying for them—generous benefits and low taxes. As I've been telling you, much of this system is on autopilot, driving us deeper and deeper into debt and closer and closer to a fiscal abyss. Our government and our political system have failed to change course and make the tough but necessary changes. I've suggested concrete ways we can address this lack of leadership. But behind this debacle stand the citizens who have demanded more for less—and rewarded the politicians who are delivering their so-called free lunch solutions. I'm betting that many more of us recognize the fiscal hole our government has dug and want to climb out and not fall back in—for the sake of our country and our children. If you've read this book, I'm betting that you agree with me and will join me.

There's another aspect of our American myth—the American

Dream: an evocation of the home of one's own and other marks of prosperity that come as a reward for hard work and enterprise. This is a dream of the American family, and a vital aspect of it is to pass our success along to others. Each generation of Americans—and each individual family—is charged with passing along a better life for those who come after us. The weakening of this intergenerational promise is the cruelest aspect of this fiscal story. In today's America, we have been robbing from the next generation, taking benefits for ourselves and deferring the payment to our children, grandchildren, and generations further. We are also reducing relative levels of federal investment in their future while they face increasing competition from abroad. I am betting that as a reader of this book you understand the dimensions of this assault on America's future and are ready to find a path for us to put us on a more prudent path, if only to give our children the opportunity for growth and success that our parents gave us.

What do we do next? At this point, more Americans should be made to understand the problem and its dimensions. That will make it hard for our government and its presiding politicians to give us the same old song and dance. If they promise us expanding vistas of universal health care, for example, without setting clear standards and goals for this program, and without making absolutely clear how we will pay for it—and what we will have to give up to pay for it—while we also reduce our tens of trillions in unfunded health care obligations, then you and I will know that the destructive fraud of promising something for nothing continues.

Are you hearing that expanded health care is "fair" and that paying for it is a simple matter of taxing the "rich"? The alarm bells are going off, aren't they? That's the same old formula that is leading us toward national decline—and you and I know we have to do better than perpetrate this massive exercise in, excuse me, BS.

Let me be a bit more precise. We have a duty as citizens to set the standards for American politics and, when our representatives present us with plans, to consider these proposals and to ask tough questions.

I'm hoping you have plenty of questions for the powers that be at this point. And remember: We can't ask these questions just once. We have to keep asking them until we get real answers and real results. Let me suggest a few for starters. Here are some of the things we ought to be asking about our elected representatives and other federal policy makers no matter what their position is and what party they are a member of:

- Have the president and key congressional leaders admitted to the American people that government has promised more than it can afford and that those promises need to be renegotiated?
- Have these leaders admitted that federal taxes must go up for more Americans than the "rich"—defined most recently as those making more than $250,000 a year—and that the longer we wait to address our large and growing deficit, the higher taxes will go?
- Are politicians still just talking about fiscal responsibility, or have they started to take action to achieve it?
- Have the conservatives with the loudest voices begun to move ever so slightly toward the center? (Pay attention to those who admit that some government spending is necessary. Note those who say that our goal should be to create a limited and effective government while keeping taxes as low as possible, rather than advocating smaller government and lower taxes. And look for conservatives who acknowledge that our economy can't grow its way out of our fiscal mess.)
- Have the liberals with the loudest voices begun to move ever so slightly toward the center? (Respect those who admit that government cannot solve all our problems. Recognize those who advocate limits on what role government can and

should play. Salute those who say we can't tax our way to prosperity and that renegotiating our current social insurance contracts is an essential component going forward.)

- Are there more elected officials calling for "nonpartisan approaches" and fewer calling for "bipartisan approaches"? (That's the kind of exhortation we need, reflecting the truth that political independents represent a large and growing portion of the American electorate.)

Their attitudes and words of leadership are important, but their actions are far more important. As our financial situation deteriorates, the bottom line is: What are our leaders doing about it? I have proposed several specific policy reforms and extraordinary processes that would help us solve our fiscal crisis, and we should hold Washington officials' feet to the fire. Here are some more questions we should ask and keep asking.

Policy Reforms

- Have government leaders recognized that spending more money and granting more tax preferences will not necessarily achieve more positive outcomes?
- Have we imposed statutory budget controls that will help to put us on a more prudent and sustainable fiscal path?
- Have we reformed the Social Security system to make it more solvent, sustainable, secure, and oriented to encourage more savings?
- Have we reformed our Medicare, Medicaid, and health care systems to control costs, provide a basic level of universal coverage, improve quality and consistency, and enhance personal responsibility and accountability?
- If a health care reform bill has passed, does it meet the tests of fiscal responsibility outlined in this book?

- Have we reformed our tax system to make it simpler, fairer, more enforceable, and more competitive, while generating adequate revenues to pay our bills and deliver on the federal government's promises?
- If we haven't done the above, have we at least formed a Fiscal Future Commission or some other strategy designed to make possible the government's promises—such as the "grand bargain" that President Obama has spoken of, a comprehensive agreement to reimpose statutory budget controls and reform entitlement programs and our health care and tax systems, where everything is on the table? If so, is the commission properly structured and empowered to achieve positive results?

Government Reforms

- The overriding question is: Have we defined and implemented an approach to transform the way the federal government does business that includes safeguards to ensure that our representatives behave in a fiscally responsible way (for example, a Baseline Review Commission)?
- Has government become more future focused and results oriented?
- Are we analyzing our nation's performance—in everything from military preparation to social services—based on clear measures of how well we have done and whether we are making progress? How do we compare to other industrialized nations on the quality and affordability of our services and the well-being of our people?
- Does the federal government finally have a comprehensive and integrated strategic plan to help guide us rationally into the future?
- Have we designed and implemented a set of key national in-

dicators to help improve performance, enhance accountability, and stimulate citizen engagement?

- Has the Pentagon begun to focus on current and future threats and put its appetite in check while improving its business practices and accountability to the public?
- Has the federal government begun to rationalize its pay and benefit programs to make them more realistic and responsible?

Political Reforms

- Is the ideological gap between the politicians and the people getting bigger or smaller?
- Have we enacted redistricting, campaign finance, and term limit reforms for federal elected offices?
- Do we have more or fewer career politicians?

In addition to asking tough questions and demanding answers, we must recognize that all of us will need to assume more responsibility for our own financial future. Eventually, the government will have to make tough choices, and when it does, the younger you are and the better off you are financially, the more you will be affected.

Finally, of course, come the questions we all should be asking ourselves: Are we doing our part to be more responsible financially? Are we also becoming more active in discharging our civic responsibilities—to make our nation's leaders more responsible and accountable?

This country has faced major challenges in the past, and we Americans have always risen to address them once we have made up our minds to do so. I believe that we will rise to meet our fiscal challenges today. That's why I called this book "Comeback America."

We don't have any time to waste. We must reexamine what the

government does and how the government does business. We must focus on the future and on achieving real results. We must be a leader in the world but also become a better partner for progress with other countries. We must work harder across our political divisions and the ideological divides in Washington to do what is right for America's and our families' futures. And yes, we must renew the power of the people and rejuvenate our democracy.

That's a broad agenda and it won't be easy, but if we start soon and put ourselves on a prudent path, the American Dream will stay on track. Our future can be better than our past. It's up to us, as Theodore Roosevelt always insisted. "It is not the critic who counts; not the man who points out how the strong man stumbles, or where the doer of deeds could have done better," he famously said. "The credit belongs to the man who is actually in the arena."

Join me and my colleagues at the Peter G. Peterson Foundation in the arena as we fight for America's future. Help us to promote responsibility and accountability today in order to create more opportunity tomorrow. Sign up under the Citizen Action section of our website at www.pgpf.org. You can also propose your own solutions and monitor the key questions outlined in this Epilogue at www.comebackamericathebook.com.

Yes, America is a great nation, but as you have discovered in this book, we are not as great as many of us think we are. It's time for us to wake up—and wake up America—to the lethal threat of our own fiscal irresponsibility. If that awakening to truth and to the national interest spreads throughout the country, it will awaken our public servants to action in Washington. We don't have any time to waste. Close the cover or turn off the reader and put this book down, fellow citizens. You've studied the problems and solutions. Now let's get to work. And as we do, let us not forget the words of John Adams: "Think of your forefathers! Think of your posterity!"

Acknowledgments

Writing a book is a major undertaking no matter the circumstances. It's an even bigger undertaking when you have another full-time job that involves being CEO of a new start-up entity—the Peter G. Peterson Foundation.

Given these realities, some loved ones make sacrifices, as quality time is lost due to the author's commitment to writing the book. In this case, Mary, my wife, is the one who has sacrificed the most, and I cannot thank her enough for her understanding and support.

Writing this book in a timely and high-quality manner required a true team effort. A number of people deserve recognition, but I have space to acknowledge only a few. First and foremost, I would like to thank Steven Strasser, who is a professor of journalism at the City University of New York. Steven's writing and editing skills were invaluable as we partnered to make this book a reality. He was not an expert on the subjects covered, but he proved to be a very quick study and his journalistic skills and layperson's perspective helped improve the readability of the book. Tim Bartlett, my editor at Random House, also lent his considerable editorial expertise and helped to ensure its timely publication. Tim's assistant,

Jessie Waters, performed countless tasks large and small to keep the book moving along.

Gail Ross was my literary agent. She provided valuable advice at every stage of the process, from helping shape my original ideas for the book to securing interest from a number of first-rate publishers, to helping me find Steve Strasser, to reading drafts of the manuscript, to flying to New York to attend marketing planning meetings. But most of all, Gail believed in the book's message and fought tirelessly to help me get it out.

Several individuals helped me in producing and referencing this book. The key players at the Peterson Foundation included Kathleen Benanti, who is my executive assistant. She spent many hours working with me writing, researching, and editing. She is my right arm at work. Pete Peterson, Gene Steuerle, Susan Tanaka, and Jackie Leo contributed their thoughts to certain topics addressed in the book. Matt Helm, Tim Roeper, and Sarah Williams all contributed considerable time and effort to researching and referencing. Others at the foundation, including Myra Sung, provided promotional or other support.

I'd also like to thank all the other people on the Random House team who worked to bring out the book, including London King and Maria Braeckel, my publicists; Avideh Bashirrad and Debbie Aroff, who put together a terrific marketing plan; Benjamin Dreyer and Evan Camfield, who handled a crash schedule without batting an eye; Paolo Pepe and Tom McKeveny, who designed a particularly striking jacket for the book; Victoria Wong, who created the book's elegant interior design; and Jennifer Hershey and Tom Perry, whose early and sustained interest in the book helped to make Random House my choice.

A number of other persons contributed their thoughts or provided other support that served to enhance the content and ensure the accuracy of the material contained in this book. They include Fred Bergsten, Steve Weisman, Gene Dodaro, Sallyanne Harper,

Dan Gordon, Tim Bowling, Chris Mihm, Helen Hsing, Marjorie Kanoff, Paul Francis, Susan Irving, Barbara Bovberg, Jim White, Butch Hinton, Beth Miller, Laura Kopelson, and Stephan Richter.

I would also like to thank Pete Peterson for his many years of commitment to promoting federal fiscal responsibility and for the opportunity that he and the other directors of the foundation (Joan Ganz-Cooney and Michael Peterson) provided me to continue my efforts to help fight for America's future as the first head of the Peter G. Peterson Foundation. Pete is a personal inspiration, a model statesperson from the business community, and a case study in the American Dream come true. Our country needs more people like him.

Finally, I'd like to thank my parents, Dave and Dot, for how they raised me and for their encouragement, along with that of others, to write this book. I have been told that it is very timely and thought-provoking. My hope is that it will help to create a movement that will make the title *Comeback America* resonate throughout this great country so that our collective future can be better than our past.

Six Simple Steps to Make Comeback America a Reality

Now that you've read this book, and hopefully recommended it to others, what else should you consider doing?

GET INFORMED AND INVOLVED

- Go to www.comebackamericathebook.com, which has a citizen action center where you can take advantage of all of the information and links noted therein.
- Be sure that you register to vote and exercise your right (and your privilege) to vote.
- Let your voice be heard on key issues in town hall meetings and other forums, through letters to the editor, articles, and opinion pieces, and otherwise. Ask tough questions based on the facts and hold your elected representatives accountable for what they do, and what they fail to do, to address the large, known, and growing challenges facing our nation.

LEAD BY EXAMPLE

- Have a personal budget and financial plan, be sure that they consider the issues outlined in this book, and stick to them.

- Plan, save, invest, preserve them for their intended purpose, avoid excess consumption, and make prudent use of credit in connection with your own financial affairs.
- Be responsible in connection with your own health and wellness (e.g., diet, exercise, personal habits).

About the Author

DAVID M. WALKER has over thirty-six years of experience in the public, private, and not-for-profit sectors and currently is president and CEO of the Peter G. Peterson Foundation. He has received three presidential appointments, one each from Reagan, Bush 41, and Clinton, including as the seventh comptroller general of the United States and CEO of the U.S. Government Accountability Office from 1998 to 2008. Walker is a frequent speaker, writer, commentator, and congressional witness and has appeared in many major publications and on a significant number of television networks, cable channels, and radio programs. He is chairman of the United Nations Independent Audit Advisory Committee, serves on several boards and advisory committees, and is a member of the Sons of the American Revolution and the Trilateral Commission.

About the Type

This book was set in Sabon, a typeface designed by the well-known German typographer Jan Tschichold (1902–74). Sabon's design is based upon the original letter forms of Claude Garamond and was created specifically to be used for three sources: foundry type for hand composition, Linotype, and Monotype. Tschichold named his typeface for the famous Frankfurt typefounder Jacques Sabon, who died in 1580.